THE SAGITTARIUS ENIGMA

Cracking the Code

ALSO BY JANE RIDDER-PATRICK

A Handbook of Medical Astrology
Shaping Your Future (Series of 12 titles)
Shaping Your Relationships (Series of 12 titles)

The Zodiac Code series

THE
SAGITTARIUS
ENIGMA

Cracking the Code

JANE RIDDER-PATRICK

MAINSTREAM
PUBLISHING
EDINBURGH AND LONDON

For my father John who could start a party —
or an argument — in an empty room.

Copyright © Jane Ridder-Patrick, 2004
All rights reserved
The moral right of the author has been asserted

First published in Great Britain in 2004 by
MAINSTREAM PUBLISHING COMPANY
(EDINBURGH) LTD
7 Albany Street
Edinburgh EH1 3UG

ISBN 1 84018 528 7

A catalogue record for this book is available
from the British Library

Typeset in Allise and Van Dijck

Printed in Great Britain by
Cox & Wyman Ltd

Contents

ONE	The Truth of Astrology	7
TWO	The Symbolism of Sagittarius	16
THREE	The Heart of the Sun	21
FOUR	The Drama of Being a Sagittarian	25
FIVE	The Sagittarius Temperament	28
SIX	Aspects of the Sun	41
SEVEN	Meeting Your Moon	48
EIGHT	Mercury – It's All in the Mind	67
NINE	Venus – At Your Pleasure	76
TEN	Famous Sagittarius Birthdays	85
ELEVEN	Finding Your Sun, Moon, Mercury and Venus Signs	94
	The Sagittarius Workbook	119
	Resources	126
	Your Sagittarian Friends	127
	Sign Summaries	128

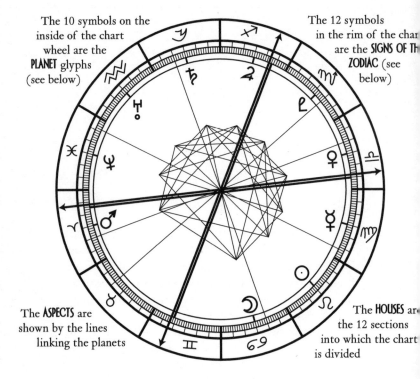

The 10 symbols on the inside of the chart wheel are the **PLANET** glyphs (see below)

The 12 symbols in the rim of the chart are the **SIGNS OF THE ZODIAC** (see below)

The **ASPECTS** are shown by the lines linking the planets

The **HOUSES** are the 12 sections into which the chart is divided

A Sample Birth Chart

Sign	Ruler	Sign	Ruler
Aries ♈	Mars ♂	Libra ♎	Venus ♀
Taurus ♉	Venus ♀	Scorpio ♏	Pluto ♇
Gemini ♊	Mercury ☿	Sagittarius ♐	Jupiter ♃
Cancer ♋	Moon ☽	Capricorn ♑	Saturn ♄
Leo ♌	Sun ☉	Aquarius ♒	Uranus ♅
Virgo ♍	Mercury ☿	Pisces ♓	Neptune ♆

ONE

The Truth of Astrology

MOST PEOPLE'S FIRST EXPERIENCE OF ASTROLOGY IS THROUGH newspapers and magazines. This is a mixed blessing for astrology's reputation – writing an astrology column to any degree of accuracy is a tough, many would say impossible, challenge. The astrologer has to try to say something meaningful about conditions that affect every single person belonging to the same sign, over a very short period of time, in a scant handful of words. The miracle is that some talented astrologers do manage to get across a tantalising whiff of the real thing and keep readers coming back for more of what most of us are hungry for – self-knowledge and reassurance about the future. The downside of the popularity of these columns is that many people think that all astrology is a branch of the entertainment industry and is limited to light-hearted fortune-telling. This is far from the truth.

What Astrology Can Offer

Serious astrology is one of the most sophisticated tools available to help us understand ourselves and the world around us. It gives us a language and a framework to examine and describe – quite literally – *anything* under the Sun, from countries to companies, from money markets to medical matters. Its most common application, however, is in helping people to understand themselves better using their own unique birth charts. Astrology has two main functions. One is to describe the traits and tendencies of whatever it is that is being examined, whether this is a state, a software company or someone's psyche. The other is to give an astonishingly accurate timetable for important changes within that entity. In the chapters that follow, we'll be using astrology to investigate the psychology of the innermost part of your personality, taking a look at what drives, inspires and motivates you.

Astrology uses an ancient system of symbols to describe profound truths about the nature of life on earth, truths that cannot be weighed and measured, but ones we recognise nevertheless, and that touch and move us at a deep level. By linking mythology and mathematics, astrology bridges the gap between our inner lives and our outer experiences, between mind and matter, between poetry and science.

Fate and Free Will

Some people think that astrology is all about foretelling the future, the implication being that everything is predestined and that we have no say in how our lives take shape. None of that is true. We are far from being helpless victims of fate. Everything that happens to us at any given time is the result of past choices. These choices may have been our own, or made by other people. They could even have been made long ago before we, or even our grandparents, were born. It is not always possible to prevent processes that were set in motion in the past from coming to their logical conclusions as events that we then have to deal with. We are, however, all free to decide how to react to whatever is presented to us at every moment of our lives.

Your destiny is linked directly with your personality because the choices you make, consciously or unconsciously, depend largely on your own natural inclinations. It is these inclinations that psychological astrology describes. You can live out every single part of your chart in a constructive or a less constructive way. For instance, if you have Aries strong in your chart, action and initiative will play a major role in your life. It is your choice whether you express yourself aggressively or assertively, heroically or selfishly, and also whether you are the doer or the done-to. Making the right choices is important because every decision has consequences – and what you give out, sooner or later, you get back. If you don't know and understand yourself, you are 'fated' to act according to instinct and how your life experiences have conditioned you. By revealing how you are wired up temperamentally, astrology can highlight alternatives to blind knee-jerk reactions, which often make existing problems worse. This self-knowledge can allow you to make more informed free-will choices, and so help you create a better and more successful future for yourself.

Astrology and Prediction

Astrology cannot predict specific events based on your birth chart. That kind of prediction belongs to clairvoyance and divination. These specialities, when practised by gifted and responsible individuals, can give penetrating insights into events that are likely to happen in the future if matters proceed along their present course.

The real benefit of seeing into the future is that if we

don't like what could happen if we carry on the way we're going, we can take steps either to prevent it or to lessen its impact. Rarely is the future chiselled out in stone. There are many possible futures. What you feed with your attention grows. Using your birth chart, a competent astrologer can map out, for years in advance, major turning points, showing which areas of your life will be affected at these times and the kind of change that will be taking place. This information gives answers to the questions that most clients ask in one way or another: 'Why me, why this and why now?' If you accept responsibility for facing what needs to be done at the appropriate time, and doing it, you can change the course of your life for the better.

Astrology and the Soul

What is sometimes called the soul and its purpose is a mystery much more profound than astrology. Most of us have experienced 'chance' meetings and apparent 'tragedies' which have affected the direction of our entire lives. There is an intelligence at work that is infinitely wiser and more powerful than the will or wishes of our small, egocentric personalities. This force, whatever name we give it – Universal Wisdom, the Inner Guide, the Self, a guardian angel – steers us into exactly the right conditions for our souls' growth. Astrology can pinpoint the turning points in the course of your destiny and describe the equipment that you have at your disposal for serving, or resisting, the soul's purpose. That equipment is your personality.

Who Are You?

You are no doubt aware of your many good qualities as well as your rather more resistible ones that you might prefer to keep firmly under wraps. Maybe you have wondered why it is that one part of your personality seems to want to do one thing while another part is stubbornly intent on doing the exact opposite. Have you ever wished that you could crack the code that holds the secrets of what makes you – and significant others – behave in the complex way you do? The good news is that you can, with the help of your astrological birth chart, sometimes known as your horoscope.

Just as surely as your DNA identifies you and distinguishes you from everyone else, as well as encoding your peculiarities and potential, your birth chart reveals the unique 'DNA fingerprinting' of your personality. This may seem a staggering claim, but it is one that those who have experienced serious astrology will endorse, so let's take a closer look at what a birth chart is.

Your Birth Chart

Your birth chart is a simplified diagram of the positions of the planets, as seen from the place of your birth, at the moment you took your first independent breath. Critics have said that astrology is obviously nonsense because birth charts are drawn up as if the Sun and all the planets moved round the Earth.

We know in our minds that the Earth moves round the Sun, but that doesn't stop us seeing the Sun rise in the east in the morning and move across the sky to set in the west in the evening. This is an optical illusion. In the same way, we know (or at least most of us know) that we are not really the centre of the universe, but that doesn't stop us experiencing ourselves as being at the focal point of our own personal worlds. It is impossible to live life in any other way. It is the strength, not weakness, of astrology that it describes from your own unique viewpoint how you, as an individual, experience life.

Erecting Your Chart

To draw up a full birth chart you need three pieces of information – the date, time and place of your birth. With your birth date alone you can find the positions of all the planets (except sometimes the Moon) to a good enough degree of accuracy to reveal a great deal of important information about you. If you have the time and place of birth, too, an astrologer can calculate your Ascendant or Rising Sign and the houses of your chart – see below. The Ascendant is a bit like the front door of your personality and describes your general outlook on life. (If you know your Ascendant sign, you might like to read more about its characteristics in the book on that sign in this series.)

The diagram on page 6 shows what a birth chart looks like. Most people find it pretty daunting at first sight but it actually breaks down into only four basic units – the planets, the signs, the aspects and the houses.

The Planets

Below is a simple list of what the planets represent.

PLANET	REPRESENTS YOUR URGE TO
☉ The Sun	express your identity
☽ The Moon	feel nurtured and safe
☿ Mercury	make connections
♀ Venus	attract what you love
♂ Mars	assert your will
♃ Jupiter	find meaning in life
♄ Saturn	achieve your ambitions
♅ Uranus	challenge tradition
♆ Neptune	serve an ideal
♇ Pluto	eliminate, transform and survive

The planets represent the main psychological drives that every single one of us has. The exact way in which we express these drives is not fixed from birth but develops and evolves throughout our lives, both consciously and unconsciously. In this book we will be examining in detail four of these planets – your Sun, Moon, Mercury and Venus. These are the bodies that are right at the heart of our solar system. They correspond, in psychological astrology, to the core of your personality and represent how you express yourself, what motivates you emotionally, how you use your mind and what brings you pleasure.

The Signs
The signs your planets are in show how you tend to express your inner drives. For example, if your Mars is in the action sign of Aries, you will assert yourself pretty directly, pulling no punches. If your Venus is in secretive Scorpio, you will attract, and also be attracted to, emotionally intense relationships. There is a summary of all of the signs on p. 128.

The Aspects
Aspects are important relationships between planets and whether your inner characteristics clash with or complement each other depends largely on whether or not they are in aspect and whether that aspect is an easy or a challenging one. In Chapter Six we'll be looking at some challenging aspects to the Sun.

The Houses
Your birth chart is divided into 12 slices, called houses, each of which is associated with a particular area of life, such as friendships, travel or home life. If, for example, you have your Uranus in the house of career, you are almost

certainly a bit of a maverick at work. If you have your Neptune in the house of partnership, you are likely to idealise your husband, wife or business partner.

The Nature of Time

Your birth chart records a moment in time and space, like a still from a movie – the movie being the apparent movement of the planets round the earth. We all know that time is something that can be measured in precise units, which are always the same, like seconds, months and centuries. But if you stop to reflect for a moment, you'll also recognise that time doesn't always feel the same. Twenty minutes waiting for a bus on a cold, rainy day can seem like a miserable eternity, while the same amount of time spent with someone you love can pass in a flash. As Einstein would say – that's relativity.

There are times in history when something significant seems to be in the air, but even when nothing momentous is happening the quality of time shifts into different 'moods' from moment to moment. Your birth chart is impregnated with the qualities of the time when you were born. For example, people who were born in the mid-to-late 1960s, when society was undergoing major disruptive changes, carry those powerful energies within them and their personalities reflect, in many ways, the turmoil of those troubled and exciting times. Now, as adults, the choices that those individuals make, based on their own inner conflicts and compulsions, will help shape the future of society for better or worse. And so it goes on through the generations.

Seed Meets Soil

There is no such thing as a good or bad chart, nor is any one sign better or worse than another. There are simply 12 different, but equally important, life focuses. It's useful to keep in mind the fact that the chart of each one of us is made up of all the signs of the zodiac. This means that we'll act out, or experience, *every* sign somewhere in our lives. It is true, however, that some individual charts are more challenging than others; but the greater the challenge, the greater the potential for achievement and self-understanding.

In gardening terms, your chart is a bit like the picture on a seed packet. It shows what you could become. If the seeds are of poppies, there's no way you'll get petunias, but external conditions will affect how they grow. With healthy soil, a friendly climate and green-fingered gardeners, the plants have an excellent chance of flourishing. With poor soil, a harsh climate or constant neglect, the seeds will be forced to struggle. This is not always a disadvantage. They can become hardy and adapt, finding new and creative ways of evolving and thriving under more extreme conditions than the plant that was well cared for. It's the same with your chart. The environment you were raised in may have been friendly or hostile to your nature and it will have done much to shape your life until now. Using the insights of astrology to affirm who you are, you can, as an adult, provide your own ideal conditions, become your own best gardener and live out more fully – and successfully – your own highest potential.

TWO

The Symbolism of Sagittarius

WE CAN LEARN A GREAT DEAL ABOUT SAGITTARIUS BY looking at the symbolism and the myths and legends associated with it. These carry more information than plain facts alone and hint at the deeper meanings and significance of the sign.

The Sagittarius glyph is an arrow with a line through its shaft, tilted up at an angle, which allows it to fly both high and wide. This reflects your tendency to think big and aim for the stars in whatever you do, as well as your love of shooting ahead at full speed into the future and the unknown. The uncertainty about how far the arrows of your thoughts or ventures could reach, or what they might meet on their travels, sends a shiver of pleasurable anticipation right through you.

The arrow, as you yourself would dearly love to do, flies onward and upward, far above the restraints and limitations of everyday life, seeming to defy, for a short while at least, the laws of gravity, before it comes back down to earth with a thud. It is the bar across the arrow shaft, symbolising the bow pulled by the archer, which reminds us that an arrow is not a free agent, but depends on forces in the material world to make it fly. That's the part – the restrictions of being earthbound – that many Sagittarians would prefer to ignore; but life won't let you. The line through the arrow shaft also refers to the division between your higher and lower nature. The challenge for you, as a Sagittarian, is to decide how and where to use your lively and restless physical and mental powers.

Sagittarius the Archer

The symbol of Sagittarius is the centaur, a strange hybrid creature with the head and torso of a human and the body of a horse. It is usually shown at full gallop, bow drawn back ready to shoot off an arrow up into the air. The horse and human fused into one show the two sides of Sagittarius that somehow, like Siamese twins, must learn to live together.

A wild horse roams free, wherever the notion takes it, with the wind in its mane and nostrils flaring, full of high spirits, kicking up its heels at the sheer joy of life. Hard to catch, until broken in it's unpredictable, and sometimes even dangerous. It's certainly highly resistant to carrying anything on its back or pulling its weight – just like the wild, freedom-loving part of Sagittarius that prefers not to be tied down and domesticated. Untamed creatures can't roam freely, though, in civilised society, which depends on agreed rules and regulations to make life fair and safe for everyone. A horse, which makes a good servant but a bad master, needs a firm rider to control it. This is where the upper half of the centaur comes in, representing the human capacity to think beyond the present moment, to see yourself as part of a community, and to recognise that there is more to life than purely selfish instinctual pleasures. As a Sagittarian, you are pulled in two directions at once. Your challenge is to find a way of taming the wild horse, representing your lust for life and desire for unbridled freedom, so that your vitality and love of adventure can be integrated with your intelligence, sense of morality and desire to aim at higher things.

Sagittarius in Myth and Legend

In Greek mythology, the half-man half-horse centaurs were a wild, unruly bunch, revelling in wine, women and debauchery, and generally creating mayhem. Their king, however, stood out from the crowd. His name was Chiron. He was a wise, kindly and highly respected healer, scholar and teacher. It was he who taught the art of healing to Asclepius, the founder of medicine. Kings sent their sons to be educated by him and he was the mentor of great heroes like Achilles and Aeneas.

One day another hero, Hercules, accidentally shot Chiron in the lower quarters with an arrow dipped in deadly poison, causing him terrible pain. Unfortunately, despite all his knowledge and experience, he wasn't able to heal himself. Worse, he couldn't die either because he was immortal. It all ended well, though. Prometheus, creator of the human race, had been tortured for years as a punishment for stealing fire from the gods to give to humans. He couldn't be released from his suffering until some immortal agreed to die in his place. Chiron was only too happy to make the exchange, as – according to some accounts– even before the poison arrow incident, he had been tired of living such a long life. So both were released from their pain. The arrow that had shot Chiron was then placed in the sky as the constellation of Sagittarius, and Chiron got his name in lights, too, in the constellation of Centaurus.

This strange story highlights several Sagittarian characteristics. One is the recurrent theme of the two strands in your nature – the wild and the wise – shown by common centaurs and their king, Chiron. The second is the luck that always seems to land in the laps of Sagittarians. No matter what ill fortune life sends you, there always seems to be a blessing disguised in it somewhere – and other people generally benefit, too.

The Ruler of Sagittarius

Each sign is ruled by a planet, which shares many of its characteristics. Sagittarius is ruled by Jupiter. Jupiter, or Zeus as he was called in Greek mythology, was king of the gods. Another of his names was Jove, which is where the word jovial comes from – an apt description of many Sagittarians. Like the centaur, he too had a double nature, this time not in his body, but in his character. On the one hand, he was the god of the law and public morality; on the other he was a shameless philanderer from whose outrageous seductions countless offspring were born. These represent the boundless vitality and creativity of Sagittarians, which often break through the constraints of everyday life. In his exploits he was closely pursued by his jealous wife Hera, the goddess of marriage, who represents the human commitments and worldly responsibilities that Sagittarians often try to duck out of. Having the luck of the gods – literally – he usually got away with his escapades. Sagittarians seem to need someone, or something, to escape from. Your adventures wouldn't be half as much fun otherwise, and also you need that very ball and chain to ground you.

The Season of Sagittarius

The month of Sagittarius is a time of celebration and hope for the future. It's the party season as Christmas approaches. Hanukkah, the Festival of Lights, falls in December and celebrates the religious freedom the Jewish people won to worship in their own way. The American holiday of Thanksgiving is held during the time of Sagittarius, on the fourth Thursday in November. This celebrates the prosperity of an abundant harvest reaped by early settlers in their new land and gratitude for the generosity of the Native American Indians without whose assistance, and wise teachings, they could not have survived. It gives thanks, too, for the freedom to follow personal beliefs, out of reach of the persecution in the Old World from which the pilgrims had fled.

THREE

The Heart of the Sun

O THE GLYPH FOR THE SUN IS A PERFECT CIRCLE WITH A DOT in the centre and symbolises our dual nature – earthly and eternal. The circle stands for the boundary of the personality, which distinguishes and separates each individual from every other individual, for it is our differences from other people that make us unique, not our similarities. The dot in the centre indicates the mysterious 'divine spark' within us and the potential for becoming conscious of who we truly are, where we have come from and what we may become.

The Meaning of the Sun
Each of your planets represents a different strand of your personality. The Sun is often reckoned to be the most important factor of your whole birth chart. It describes your sense of identity, and the sign that the Sun was in when you were born, your Sun sign, along with its house position and any aspects to other planets, shows how you express and develop that identity.

Your Role in Life

Each of the signs is associated with certain roles that can be played in an infinite number of ways. Take one of the roles of Aries, which is the warrior. A warrior can cover anything from Attila the Hun, who devastated vast stretches of Europe with his deliberate violence, to an eco-warrior, battling to save the environment. The role, warrior, is the same; the motivation and actions are totally different. You can live out every part of your personality in four main ways – as creator, destroyer, onlooker or victim. How you act depends on who you choose to be from the endless variations possible from the symbolism of each of your planets, but most particularly your Sun. And you do have a choice; not all Geminis are irresponsible space cadets nor is every Scorpio a sex-crazed sadist. This book aims to paint a picture of what some of your choices might be and show what choices, conscious or unconscious, some well-known people of your sign have made.

Your upbringing will have helped shape what you believe about yourself and out of those beliefs comes, automatically, behaviour to match. For example, if you believe you are a victim, you will behave like one and the world will happily oblige by victimising you. If you see yourself as a carer, life will present you with plenty to care for – and often to care about, too. If you identify yourself as an adventurer, you'll spot opportunities at every corner. If you're a winner, then you'll tend to succeed. Shift the way that you see yourself and your whole world shifts, too.

Your Vocation

Your Sun describes your major life focus. This is not always a career. As the poet Milton said: 'They also serve who only stand and wait.' It is impossible to tell from your Sun sign exactly what your calling is – there are people of all signs occupied in practically every area of life. What is important is not so much *what* you do, but the way that you do it and it is this – how you express yourself – that your Sun describes. If you spend most of your time working at an occupation or living in a situation where you can't give expression to the qualities of your Sun, or which forces you to go against the grain of your Sun's natural inclinations, then you're likely to live a life of quiet, or possibly even noisy, desperation.

On Whose Authority

Your personality, which your birth chart maps, is like a sensitive instrument that will resonate only to certain frequencies – those that are similar to its own. Your Sun shows the kind of authority that will strike a chord with you, either positively or negatively, because it is in harmony with yours. It can show how you relate to people in authority, especially your father. (It is the Moon that usually shows the relationship with your mother and home.) In adult life it can throw light onto the types of bosses you are likely to come across, and also how you could react to them. It is a major part of the maturing process to take responsibility for expressing your own authority wisely. When you do so, many of your problems with external authorities diminish or even disappear.

In a woman's chart the Sun can also describe the kind of husband she chooses. This is partly because, traditionally, a husband had legal authority over his wife. It is also because, especially in the early years of a marriage, many women choose to pour their energies into homemaking and supporting their husbands' work in the world, rather than their own, and so his career becomes her career. As a

Sagittarian, you may find that your father, boss or husband shows either the positive or negative traits of Sagittarius or, as is usually the case, a mixture of both – enterprising, wise and generous or irresponsible, pontificating and tactless.

Born on the Cusp

If you were born near the beginning or end of Sagittarius, you may know that your birthday falls on the cusp, or meeting point, of two signs. The Sun, however, can only be in one sign or the other. You can find out for sure which sign your Sun is in by checking the tables on pp.97–8.

FOUR

The Drama of Being a Sagittarian

EACH SIGN IS ASSOCIATED WITH A CLUSTER OF ROLES THAT HAVE their own core drama or storyline. Being born is a bit like arriving in the middle of an ongoing play and slipping into a certain part. How we play our characters is powerfully shaped in early life by having to respond to the input of the other actors around us — the people that make up our families and communities. As the play of our lives unfolds, we usually become aware that there are themes which tend to repeat themselves. We may ask ourselves questions like 'Why do I always end up with all the work / caught up in fights / with partners who mistreat me / in dead-end jobs / successful but unhappy . . .?' or whatever. Interestingly, I've found that people are less likely to question the wonderful things that happen to them again and again.

The good news is that once we recognise the way we have been playing our roles, we can then use our free-will choice to do some creative rescripting, using the same character in more constructive scenarios. Even better news is that if we change, the other people in our dramas have got to make some alterations, too. If you refuse to respond to the same old cues in the customary ways, they are going to have to get creative, too.

A key role of Sagittarius is the adventurer. An adventurer is ready, at the drop of a hat, to jump into some kind of hazardous enterprise, often just for the sheer fun of it, or simply because the opportunity presents itself and it seems too good to miss. Adventurers are willing to trust their luck, and often to push it to the limits, in the hope that the risk will pay off, resulting in some kind of gain – preferably without the pain. The dream is of discovering vast wealth, or knowledge, or position by pushing back the frontiers and venturing into unknown, and often dangerous, territory. These frontiers can be geographical, social, mental or spiritual. An adventurer is a gambler, a willing soldier of fortune, ready to risk all on the turn of a card. He or she is open to accepting whatever life sends along but, at the same time, keeps alive the faith that somewhere, just over the next rainbow, are riches beyond measure.

Some adventurers will use dubious means to achieve their ends. By trickery, barefaced effrontery and sheer audacity, they'll try to push through their projects at the minimum expense to themselves. Sometimes, though, they get their come-uppance, but, like Shakespeare's loveable rogue Falstaff, they'll then usually just pick themselves up with a laugh, shake themselves down and, undaunted, look around for the next sure-fire scheme. There is something irrepressible about chancers and rascals of this kind. No matter how many times their plans go wrong, or that which glitters turns out to be merely fool's gold, they don't stay deflated for long.

When they come back from their adventures, foreign, financial or fiscal, they can dine out for months on travellers' tales, which both entertain and instruct. Because they don't stick to the tourist routes, our intrepid explorers will have much to tell of unknown territory and its potential. And if they come back empty-handed, they bring back treasure of another kind – a wealth of experience, even if it's only in cautionary tales.

Other Sagittarius roles are the guru, coach, preacher, philosopher, traveller and speculator. All of these explore possibilities and expand the consciousness of those involved. How you choose to see your role will determine your behaviour. The following chapter describes some typical Sagittarian behaviour. Remember, though, that there is no such thing as a person who is all Sagittarius and nothing but Sagittarius. You are much more complicated than that and other parts of your chart will modify, or may even seem to contradict, the single, but central, strand of your personality which is your Sun sign. These other sides of your nature will add colour and contrast and may restrict or reinforce your basic Sagittarian identity. They won't, however, cancel out the challenges you face as a Sagittarius.

FIVE

The Sagittarius Temperament

A ROLLING STONE, IT IS SAID, GATHERS NO MOSS. MOSS, fortunately, is usually the last thing that interests you. Experience is what you're after – of just about anything that you haven't seen, been or done before. You're hungry to explore and understand life. You want to embrace all of it and find out where you belong in the great scheme of things.

New Worlds to Conquer

For you, life's a never-ending journey, every day a new adventure, and each step on the way a leap of faith. There is nothing closed about you. You rush out to meet and greet events with arms and heart open wide. You long for the freshness and excitement of the unknown and the unexplored. Faraway places are constantly beckoning. The grass may not always be greener on the other side of the fence, but you're itching to check it out just in case . . . As the foreign intrigues you more than the familiar, you have little interest in restricting yourself to what's in your own backyard. And being so democratic, you're rarely snobbish.

You're far too busy finding out about people to waste time judging them.

The Travel Bug

Most Sagittarians are enthusiastic globetrotters, with suitcase or rucksack packed at the ready. Others operate more on the intellectual level, chasing new knowledge, information and points of view, while the philosophically inclined fire off their intuitive arrows to probe the laws that run the universe. Many do all three. As you're on a perpetual quest, standing still doesn't feature large on your journey plan. You've scarcely reached a goal before another one lures you off to pastures new. Robert Louis Stevenson, who had his Venus in Sagittarius, wrote, 'To travel hopefully is a better thing than to arrive' and, 'I travel not to go anywhere, but to go, I travel for travel's sake. The great affair is to move.' Those are sentiments dear to the hearts of most Sagittarians.

Off at Tangents

With your low boredom threshold, you're restless and easily side-tracked. When the promise of adventure appears on the horizon, you're apt, on a sudden impulse, to shoot off after it in hot pursuit, and follow where it leads. This tendency to go off at tangents means that you're frequently late for appointments and mealtimes are moveable feasts.

Upward and Onward

With unquenchable hope and optimism, you look forward expectantly with little fear of the future. Frank Sinatra's gravestone reads 'The Best Is Yet to Come'. Your trust in life is contagious, inspiring others by your uplifting example. No matter how many disappointments come your way, you always seem to be able to bounce back, with spirits buoyant and exuberance unabated.

Don't Tie Me Down

Sagittarians are the cowboys – and cowgirls – of the zodiac. Personal freedom is essential for you. You hate restraints, mental, physical or emotional, and want to feel free to roam, and to come and go as you please. You plunge whole-heartedly into whatever you do and prefer to do only what you believe in. Being bossed around, or having demands made on you, is not to your liking. Too much – indeed sometimes any – responsibility feels like a crushingly heavy burden. When caged or kennelled, you'll almost always manage to find an escape route. One Sagittarian man I know who had an overbearing wife spent most of his married life on permanent night shift.

Material World

There is a saying: 'Put your trust in God and remember to lock your car.' It's the second part that you have trouble with. You can be trusting to the point of foolhardiness and, being so intent on chasing rainbows, practical considerations are easily overlooked. Organisation and attending to everyday maintenance are not your top priority, nor your forte, either. Life's too short to bother about details and you may try to ignore or avoid these petty irritants, so you can be absent-minded or neglectful about dreary duties. As for long-term planning – you're happy to leave that in the lap of the gods. If you do get round to doing your share of the work, you can be pretty slapdash and clumsy and it may take time to learn that a job is not finished until you've tidied up – though you're not averse to lecturing others on how to do things properly.

Risk Management

With blind faith, you'll jump right into whatever interesting speculation presents itself, as you love a good gamble. Trusting your luck and taking risks sets your spirits soaring, for you can bear, and even enjoy, uncertainty more than any other sign. Safety scarcely features on your list of considerations. You go forward expecting miracles and – exasperatingly for those who watch and wonder – when you're around, they frequently happen. Some Sagittarians are blatant opportunists and use people shamelessly, spotting those who can help them on their way and dropping them when they're no longer useful. Despite this, you're rarely guilty of what you would consider deceit or guile – you're too upfront for that – and almost never hurt others deliberately, as you haven't a single malicious bone in your body, unless Scorpio plays a prominent role in your chart.

Hope Springs Eternal

A Sagittarian speciality is cooking up sure-fire schemes for getting something quickly – like money, health, promotion, a bit of nooky or a place in heaven – but you can be careless and over-optimistic, overreaching yourself and misjudging situations. When your schemes and gambles don't pay off, you're usually a good sport and seldom sulk or brood. As your sense of dignity isn't highly developed, losing is no big deal. You'll just pick yourself up with a laugh, shrug off your problems and charge on after the next hopeful venture, irrepressible, like Del Boy in *Only Fools and Horses*.

Move It!

As you itch to be mobile, you'll use planes, trains and ships as extensions of your body, to reach sooner the places you want to be and see. While you may have a destination in mind, you'll rarely stick to the itinerary and, as you prefer to be in the fast lane, fast cars and fast living are often your style. Travelling with a Sagittarian at the wheel is usually a white-knuckle ride. The actor Sir Ralph Richardson was still roaring about on his motorbike until well into his 70s. With all your boisterous energy, you probably love sport and the great outdoors. Moving your muscles, especially those of the hips and thighs, gives you a chance to express your exuberance in physical activity. You're often good at games where speed, chase, distance and fair play are important.

Splashing the Cash

With your unbridled zest for life, you like to do things big. Your motto is: Everything to Excess. Being open-handed with advice and resources, you can be generous to the point of recklessness. You'll often pick up bills and tip extravagantly. Money you'll spend rashly, as soon as you get it, in fact often before you get it. You may promise, in the heat of the moment, more than you can later deliver – money, love everlasting, to be somewhere tomorrow at noon. As you live so much for the moment, you can genuinely forget all about it when that moment has passed and be puzzled when people get cross. You've also a hidden, and usually completely unconscious, miserly streak which surfaces from time to time, when the spectre of hard reality confronts you and reminds you it won't go away.

Bring on the Clowns

Most Sagittarians are pleasure-loving party animals with a pronounced sense of fun. Sometimes this means horseplay and clowning around. Being totally unselfconscious, you don't mind making a fool of yourself even if it embarrasses family and friends, who'll melt into the crowd and pretend you don't belong to them. There's part of you that never fully grows up – or grows old either – no matter how respectable your place in the community. A Sagittarian doctor friend was dared to go shopping with a pair of his wife's knickers over his head. Without a moment's hesitation, that's exactly what he did, and thoroughly enjoyed the startled reactions he caused. Being gregarious, you're a good mixer and the very best of company. You're often an excellent raconteur, too, and as you're capable of exaggerating wildly, at every telling your stories could become more elaborately embroidered and entertaining.

Saying It How It Is

Unless you have plenty of water in your chart, sensing what others are feeling doesn't come easily. Subtlety is not your strong point, so you can be frank and outspoken, sometimes to the point of brutality. It's almost as if you stumble over people's 'Keep Out' signs and can't help trespassing. It's hard for you to keep secrets and to understand why anyone would want to be reticent or shy. Your intentions are honourable, but you don't see the point of flattery and can innocently deflate pomposity and trample all over people's most sensitive corns. Your chronic foot-in-the-mouth disease and tact deficit come from speaking first and thinking later. You're usually totally unaware of your gaffes, and the hurts they are causing, as they come about through your desire to be truthful and not from deliberate cruelty. After you've dropped one of your many clangers, it's best not to try to explain, other than to say sorry, as you can so easily end up adding insult to injury by helpfully explaining *exactly* why you said what you did. It would be a generous gesture to your loved ones if you'd work at noticing the consequences of your actions, and reflect on the feedback you are given.

Temper, Temper

If you feel you've been taken for a ride, or a slur has been made on your integrity, or are even just a bit grumpy, you'll erupt like Vesuvius, showering blistering sarcasm on often innocent bystanders. Your thunder and lightning and sound effects are impressive, but terrifying to the timid. While you recover your temper quickly and are all sunshine after showers – and don't hold grudges – the same can't be said of the more sensitive souls who suffer horribly from your fall-out and can smart from the wounds for months and even years to follow. A thick skin comes in useful around a Sagittarian.

Darkness and Despair

Underneath that bubbly and sometimes manic exterior, there can be a touch of sadness and despair and, sometimes, even bitterness. Secretly you feel godlike, and it's hard for you to come to terms with the fact that you're also an ordinary human being who will one day die. The thrill of the chase excites you, so you're always running towards, or away from, something but, with time, you could come to realise that you can travel the wide world over and still not escape the limitations, loneliness and frustration that are part of life's lot. Your true search is actually for freedom of spirit and the pursuit of wisdom. When you redirect your energy to mental and spiritual aims, the impulse to rove the world changes into a desire to explore the riches of the inner world. Wisdom comes when you accept that true freedom comes only by working within the laws of nature, inner and outer, higher and lower.

The Meaning of Life

Even if you're poorly educated, you'll keep yourself well-informed and will rarely pass up on an opportunity to learn. Being open-minded, your views and ways of thinking can be strikingly unconventional. You've got a strong sense that life has got some kind of significance and purpose – and you want to find out what it is. Off-the-peg beliefs are not for you. You see life like a giant jigsaw puzzle, but the pieces are scattered, and the box lid is missing. So you gradually build up your own philosophy, fitting together segments of your own experience to guesstimate what the big picture might be. You don't see facts and events in isolation, but as somehow significantly connected to society, and to life as a whole. Using imagination rather than logic, you can turn a fact into theory at lightning speed. Unfortunately, you are also given to sweeping judgements and can jump to wildly wrong conclusions if you're on unfamiliar territory. It pays to check the facts if you want to be taken seriously.

Crusading Zeal

You're an active philosopher and want to put what you believe into practice. So you translate your vision of the purpose of life into codes of conduct and moral standards, and then try to convert everyone else to your point of view. Many Sagittarians would rather argue than eat, and a few can become garrulous bores when they get on to their pet topics. Your convictions are strong, but can be changeable. You tub-thump your beliefs as if they were gospel and carved out of granite, but if you have a change of heart, you'll promote your new ones with just as much fervour. Jane Fonda was a voluble opponent of the Vietnam War. She was equally fervent about exercise and then found Christianity. Some will go to extraordinary lengths to make sure their guidance is heeded. Even death is no hindrance. Walt Disney made a film just before he died, to be played to the directors of his company, telling them what he expected of them, and saying that he'd be seeing them . . .

Believe Me!

You're a mass of contradictions: you've no time for dogma but can be breathtakingly dogmatic yourself. You are liberal-minded but intolerant of others' views when they differ from your own. Some get fanatical and lather themselves into froths of righteous indignation and missionary zeal. When this happens, it's usually because they have underlying doubts. You are also capable of indulging in 'do as I say, not as I do' hypocrisy when your passions get the better of your principles. And when your head loses out to your hindquarters, you'll preach all the harder and faster, like a television evangelist caught with his trousers down and his fingers in the till.

Sagittarius at Work

Sagittarians need adventure, excitement, freedom and opportunities to improvise. A job where you can get out and about and visit new places and meet new people is ideal. Being stuck alone at a desk all day in a windowless back room, doing repetitive tasks, is your sure-fire way to depression. Publishing, preaching, education, coaching, travel and philosophy are all fields you could do well in. You're a born entrepreneur, as you're quick to spot opportunities and gaps in the market. Speculation of any kind is right up your street, and when you learn to tell the difference between true intuition and wild, extravagant fantasy, your gambles could pay off handsomely. Learning to discipline yourself to stick to schedules and deadlines, and to buckle down to restrictions, is well-nigh impossible but if you go halfway to meeting them, the sky's the limit to what you can achieve.

The Greatest Show in Town

There's no business like show business to bring out your best. You don't have to go on the stage or in front of a camera to perform. That you do instinctively.

You're a first-class promoter, because your dramatic style of delivery and enthusiasm can make people believe in miracles. The snake-oil salesmen that used to roll into town in the old Wild West and sell cures for every ill – then move on swiftly – must have had Sagittarius strong in their charts. Public relations is also an excellent field, as you've a knack of knowing, and getting on with, everyone and can dream up over-the-top publicity stunts that have everyone queuing up for your product. Your enthusiasm is contagious; you'll be the one in the office lifting spirits and raising morale on a cloudy day. This makes you an excellent teacher, guide or guru, as you can spot the potential in students that they didn't know they had and motivate them to give of their best. You have a remarkable eye for opportunities and you're miles ahead of the crowd in sensing the direction in which things are going, and what could take off. Often you'll promote it and help make it happen. Sagittarius is called the lucky sign. Your good fortune is usually linked to your intuitive hunches and uncanny sense of timing, plus the brazen approach and high-risk tactics that leave others open-mouthed. In your enthusiasm, you've a tendency to rush on to the next exciting project before you've finished the current one, so can find yourself overburdened and in a complete muddle, hoping, or expecting, that someone else will mop up after you.

Sagittarius and Health

Sagittarians are usually endowed with abundant vitality. Life seldom defeats you for long. Because of your positive attitude, you tend to bounce back quickly from any illness that does come to plague you, and you're likely to be still active and enthusiastic long after your contemporaries have become fused to their armchairs. Sagittarius rules the hips and thighs, the main means of locomotion. Psychologically, these are associated with moving forward. Health troubles in these areas could be linked with feeling stuck and unable to move on. Sciatica and sports injuries, especially to the hamstrings, are common. Many Sagittarians are naturally sporty, which keeps you fit. Any exercise that uses the big muscles of the buttocks and thighs – like football, rugby, riding, dancing, skiing, skating and cycling – is particularly good for you.

Squandering Your Energy

You don't feel at home crammed in the restrictions of a body, so you may neglect to feed and water yours regularly and, as socialising can be your way of life, it's all too easy to over-indulge in food and alcohol, which can play havoc with your liver. The chest area is sometimes a weak point, leading to infections and other lung and respiratory complaints. Dissipating your energy by having too many projects on the go at the one time can sometimes lead to lack of coordination and nervous exhaustion. A few good nights' sleep, and putting your mind in neutral for a while, will soon have you back on your feet again.

Being confined or inactive with no hope of change in the future can plunge you into depression. Again, change your circumstances and the melancholy should lift quickly. You do tend to be rather accident-prone, but your speciality is the spectacular lucky escape. I know several Sagittarians who, when driving too fast, have lost control of their cars at peak times on busy roads. Miraculously, for those few seconds of potential disaster, no other vehicles were around. Others have run into hedges and ditches and stepped out unharmed. I wouldn't recommend you push your luck, though.

Sagittarius in Love

Commitment equals claustrophobia for some Sagittarians. The notion of cutting down your options to only one can feel like a step too far. Yet part of you hankers for stability and, given the right conditions, you have the capacity for enduring love and loyalty. In relationships, your greatest challenge is to find a way of reconciling your swashbuckling wanderlust with your sense of morality and fairness. Wise Sagittarians recognise that total freedom is a fantasy. You're happy to accept a few limitations – especially around extra-marital adventures – provided you can channel your restlessness into different areas. It's a bit like driving and sticking to the Highway Code. As long as you keep within certain limits, you'll keep your license, and there's still an almost endless variety of vehicles and routes you can take. Some Sagittarians, though, refuse to compromise and remain committed philanderers all their lives. One I know feels it is his mission to romp through the marriage beds of Europe, testing them out for stability. The marriages that is, not the beds.

Faithful or Fancy Free?

You can't help noticing prospects and opportunities. So, even if you're faithfully and happily wedded, in your imagination you'll still wander. These fine romances are best kept locked up in the privacy of your own head. A partner is unlikely to appreciate a running report on your current passing fancy. You're rarely jealous and are more than happy for your partner to have an independent life outside of the relationship. That way both of you can stay interesting to each other. With new things to talk about, there's much less chance of boredom setting in. You're an exhilarating companion, tolerant, understanding, supportive and tremendous fun to be with. It's important that your partner can stimulate your active mind, and share at least some of your wide-ranging interests. Ideally, your partner is also your best friend. Sagittarians are usually highly sexed. Your biggest erogenous zone is your imagination, so the most direct route to your libido is through erotic images. You'll enjoy an energetic and lively sex life with a partner who works creatively with your fantasies of untried possibilities, and who never allows you to feel that you can know them completely.

SIX

Aspects of the Sun

PLANETS, JUST LIKE PEOPLE, CAN HAVE IMPORTANT RELATIONSHIPS with each other. These relationships are called aspects. Aspects to your Sun from any other planet can influence your personality markedly. The most powerful effects come with those from the slower-moving planets – Saturn, Uranus, Neptune or Pluto. Sometimes they can alter your ideas about yourself and your behaviour patterns so much that you may not feel at all typical of your sign in certain areas of your life.

Check if your birth date and year appear in the various sections below to find out if one or more of these planets was aspecting the Sun when you were born. Only the so-called challenging aspects have been included. These are formed when the planets are together, opposite or at right angles to each other in the sky.

Unfortunately, because space is restricted, other aspects have been left out, although they have similar effects to those described below and, for the same reason, a few dates will inevitably have been missed out, too. (You can find out for sure whether or not your Sun is aspected at my website www.janeridderpatrick.com) If your Sun has no aspects to Saturn, Uranus, Neptune or Pluto, you're more likely to be a typical Sagittarian.

Some well-known Sagittarians with challenging aspects to their Suns appear below. You can find more in the birthday section at the end of the book.

Sun in Sagittarius in Aspect with Saturn

If you were born between 1956 and 1958 or 1986 and 1988, whether or not your birthday is listed below, you are likely to feel the influence of Saturn on your Sun.

22 November–1 December in: 1935, 1942, 1948, 1956, 1963–4, 1971, 1977–8, 1985 and 1994

2–11 December in: 1936, 1942–3, 1949, 1957, 1965, 1972, 1978, 1986 and 1995

12–22 December in: 1937, 1943, 1950, 1958, 1966, 1973, 1979, 1988 and 1995–6

Woody Allen	General George Custer	Jane Fonda
Donny Osmond	Joanna Trollope	Andy Williams

Being acknowledged by the establishment, or recognised as an authority in your field, is what you aspire to. You have a powerful ambition to prove yourself and to make something of your life, often combined with a nagging sense of not being quite good enough. Underneath your fun-loving exterior, it may be hard for you to let your hair down and enjoy yourself, as you're always looking over your shoulder to check whether or not you're being judged and disapproved of.

Your parents may have been overly strict, or controlling. Alternatively, they could have done their duty in an exemplary way, but had little time, or few resources, to support your developing sense of self. You probably feel that you're on your own and just have to get on with it. Jane Fonda's irascible father paid her scant attention, and her mother committed suicide when Jane was 13. This early lack of support, or burden of other people's expectations, can be a great advantage because what you have, and have become, will have been worked for and earned by you, and you alone. Women with this aspect are often attracted to men who are old, cold or workaholic, or who are high-achieving pillars of society.

You may have an attitude problem towards authority, often because you'd like to be the one calling the shots. Often you will look for approval from others but, until you yourself set the goals and standards for who you want to be, and what you want to achieve, you'll always be hostage to other people's opinions. With self-discipline, determination and hard work, slowly, but surely, you will have the satisfaction of accomplishing whatever you set your sights on.

Sun in Sagittarius in Aspect with Uranus

If you were born between 1981 and 1988, whether or not your birthday is listed below, you are likely to feel the influence of Uranus on your Sun.

22 November–1 December in: 1941–4, 1961–4 and 1981–4
2–11 December in: 1944–7, 1963–6 and 1983–6
12–22 December in: 1946–9, 1965–8 and 1986–9

Ada Byron	Billy Connolly	Walt Disney
Bette Midler	Britney Spears	Steven Spielberg

Whatever else you might be, you're unlikely to be dull. You're a mould-breaker, and may take huge delight in shocking people and sticking two fingers up at convention. Billy Connolly's outrageous humour deflates pomposity and slices through social niceties. Unless you have some tactful strands woven through your chart, your outspokenness and natural inclination to react against authority – just because it's there – may lead to run-ins with bosses or traditionalists. You need almost unlimited freedom to do your own thing. At 19, Steven Spielberg claimed an empty trailer in a film studio and, without authorisation, set up shop. By 20, through talent and cheeky free enterprise, he had become a professional director. You function best when working on new and exciting projects, so when the novelty wears off, and a job becomes humdrum or too successful, you'll tend to leave, or provoke situations that force you to go. Taking on frequent short-term challenges, rather than a career structure that stretches yawningly towards a serenely dull retirement, usually suits you best.

Social issues concern you and you'll have unconventional, and often controversial, solutions to society's ills. You can see straight to the heart of injustice and inequalities, and are probably a gifted innovator and inventor. Many of your ideas that seem oddball today will be part of mainstream thinking in the future. Lord Byron's daughter Ada wrote a computer programme prototype – in 1843; in 1979 the US Department of Defense named a software language in her honour. Your father may have been unusual, or possibly even not there for you as you were growing up. Steven Spielberg often portrays fathers in his films as reluctant, absent, or irresponsible. Being tied down rarely appeals to you either. You're more likely to be comfortable in relationships that are unconventional, or allow you plenty of freedom.

Sun in Sagittarius in Aspect with Neptune

If you were born between 1970 and 1984, whether or not your birthday is listed below, you are likely to feel the influence of Neptune on your Sun.

22 November–1 December in: 1927–33 and 1969–76
2–11 December in: 1932–8 and 1974–80
12–22 December in: 1936–42 and 1979–85

Woody Allen	Jane Austen	Sai Baba
Frances Hodgson Burnett	Judi Dench	Dionne Warwick

As there is something rather elusive about you, you are hard to pin down, either physically or emotionally. It's not always easy for other people to see the real you behind the image of who they think you are. In fact, it's not always easy for you to know who you are either. Your sensitivity and sympathy for other people's suffering and distress makes you reach out to help spontaneously, but beware of being taken in by hard-luck stories. You can tune in to other people's dreams and yearnings and intuitively give the impression that you can satisfy them. This could make you a talented actor, orator, carer and healer or – if you've a mind to it – con artist.

There may be a strongly spiritual or devotional side to your nature and you may prefer to daydream rather than face the harsh and often disappointing outside world. Your task is to find some way of bringing your escapist fantasies down to earth and into everyday life, as Jane Austen did with her novels like *Pride and Prejudice* and *Mansfield Park*. You may idealise your father, but feel that he is just out of reach. Alternatively, you could find him rather ineffectual, or feel that way yourself – Woody Allen has practically made a career out of his neuroses. Women with this aspect are often drawn to men who are wounded, unavailable or in need of fixing. Your vitality is easily sapped, but regular retreats from everyday reality will soon have you bouncing back to normal; excursions into alcohol or comfort foods, however, are not the answer, as you are prone to allergies, addictions and just plain overdoing it.

Sun in Sagittarius in Aspect with Pluto

Sagittarians born between 1996 and 2008 are likely to feel the influence of Pluto on their Suns.

22 November–1 December in: 1955–62
2–11 December in: 1960–7
11–22 December in: 1965–71

Roberta Close	Walt Disney	Otto Dix
Milton Erickson	Sinead O'Connor	Edith Piaf

Your deep-seated suspicion that something dangerous lurks round every corner makes you quietly watchful. Your determination is formidable. When you make up your mind to push through some vision or scheme, you will keep at it no matter what the odds. Even if, like Edith Piaf, life sends you to hell and back, you are a survivor and can come out of tight corners stronger and more powerful than before. Pluto's agenda is to eliminate anything that is outworn, rotten or toxic. Your task is to re-evaluate what you believe about yourself, and your world, and to inspire others to do the same. You are a force to be reckoned with, and can transform the world around you for good or ill. The renowned hypnotherapist Milton Erickson had great success in helping psychotics, using his powerful method for transforming destructive beliefs. This formed the basis of neurolinguistic programming (NLP).

You may find yourself in relationships involving intense power struggles; some of them provoked by your attitude, conscious or unconscious, of 'nobody pushes me around'. Your work may take you into areas dealing with sex, secrets, death, transformation or the use or misuse of power. The artist Otto Dix is best-known for his gut-wrenching depictions of the horrors of war.

You may have a sense of being unacceptable in some way. This simply comes from the intuition you're likely to go through some major transformations, where you leave outworn parts of your old life behind. This is a cause for celebration, not fear. Your changes are unlikely to be as dramatic, though, as that of Roberta Close, 'the most beautiful woman in Brazil', who was born male and was finally allowed to have a sex-change operation to become who she felt she truly was.

SEVEN

Meeting Your Moon

⟩ THE GLYPH FOR THE MOON IS THE SEMI-CIRCLE OR CRESCENT. It is a symbol for the receptiveness of the soul and is associated with feminine energies and the ebb and flow of the rhythms of life. In some traditions it represents the gateway to paradise and the realms of bliss.

The Sun and Moon are the two complementary poles of your personality, like yang and yin, masculine and feminine, active and reflective, career and home, father and mother. The Moon comes into its own as a guide at night, the time of sleeping consciousness. It also has a powerful effect on the waters of the earth. Likewise, the Moon in your birth chart describes what you respond to instinctively and feel 'in your waters', often just below the level of consciousness. It is your private radar system, sending you messages via your body responses and feelings, telling you whether a situation seems safe or scary, nice or nasty. Feelings provide vital information about circumstances in and around you. Ignore them at your peril; that will lead you into emotional, and sometimes even physical, danger. Eating disorders tend to be associated with being out of touch with, or neglecting, the instincts and the body, both of which the Moon describes.

Extraordinary though it might seem to those who are emotionally tuned in, some people have great difficulty in knowing what they are feeling. One simple way is to pay attention to your body. Notice any sensations that attract your attention. Those are linked to your feelings. Now get a sense of whether they are pleasant or unpleasant, then try to put a more exact name to what those feelings might be. Is it sadness, happiness, fear? What is it that they are trying to tell you? Your Moon hints at what will strongly activate your feelings. Learning to trust and decode this information will help make the world seem – and be – a safer place.

The Moon represents your drive to nurture and protect yourself and others. Its sign, house and aspects describe how you respond and adapt emotionally to situations and what feeds you, in every sense of the word. It gives information about your home and home life and how you experienced your mother, family and childhood, as well as describing your comfort zone of what feels familiar – the words 'family' and 'familiar' come from the same source. It shows, too, what makes you feel secure and what could comfort you when you're feeling anxious. Your Moon describes what moves and motivates you powerfully at the deepest instinctual level and indicates what is truly the 'matter' in – or with – your life.

Knowing children's Moon signs can help parents and teachers better understand their insecurities and respect their emotional make-up and needs, and so prevent unnecessary hurt, or even harm, to sensitive young lives. It's all too easy to expect that our children and parents should have the same emotional wiring as we do, but that's rarely how life works. Finding our parents' Moon signs can be a real revelation. It can often help us understand where they are coming from, what they need and why they react to us in the way they do. Many of my clients have been able to find the understanding and compassion to forgive their parents when they realised that they were doing their very best with the emotional resources available to them.

In relationships it is important that your Moon's requirements are met to a good enough extent. For example, if you have your Moon in Sagittarius you must have adventure, freedom and the opportunity to express your beliefs. If being with your partner constantly violates these basic needs, you will never feel secure and loved and the relationship could, in the long term, undermine you. However, if your Moon feels too comfortable, you will never change and grow. The art is to get a good working balance between support and challenge.

A man's Moon sign can show some of the qualities he will unconsciously select in a wife or partner. Some of the others are shown in his Venus sign. Many women can seem much more like their Moon signs than their Sun signs, especially if they are involved in mothering a family and being a support system for their husbands or partners. It is only at the mid-life crisis that many women start to identify more with the qualities of their own Suns rather than living that out through their partners' ambitions. Similarly men tend to live out the characteristics of their Moon signs through their wives and partners until mid-life, often quite cut off from their own feelings and emotional responses. If a man doesn't seem at all like his Moon sign, then check out the women in his life. There's a good chance that his wife, mother or daughter will show these qualities.

Your Moon can be in any sign, including the same one as your Sun. Each sign belongs to one of the four elements: Fire, Earth, Air or Water. The element of your Moon can give you a general idea of how you respond to new situations and what you need to feel safe and comforted. We all become anxious if our Moon's needs are not being recognised and attended to. We then, automatically, go into our personal little rituals for making ourselves feel better. Whenever you are feeling distressed, especially when you are way out of your comfort zone in an unfamiliar situation, do something to feed and soothe your Moon. You're almost certain to calm down quickly.

Fire Moons

If you have a fire Moon in Aries, Leo or Sagittarius, your first response to any situation is to investigate in your imagination the possibilities for drama, excitement and self-expression. Feeling trapped by dreary routine in an ordinary humdrum life crushes you completely. Knowing that you are carrying out a special mission feeds your soul. To you, all the world's a stage and a voyage of discovery. Unless you are at the centre of the action playing some meaningful role, anxiety and depression can set in. To feel secure, you have to have an appropriate outlet for expressing your spontaneity, honourable instincts and passionate need to be of unique significance. The acknowledgement, appreciation and feedback of people around you are essential, or you don't feel real. Not to be seen and appreciated, or to be overlooked, can feel like a threat to your very existence.

Earth Moons

If you have an earth Moon in Taurus, Virgo or Capricorn, you'll respond to new situations cautiously and practically. Rapidly changing circumstances where you feel swept along and out of control are hard for you to cope with. You need time for impressions to sink in. Sometimes it is only much later, after an event has taken place, that you become sure what you felt about it. Your security lies in slowing down, following familiar routines and rituals, even if they are a bit obsessive, and focusing on something, preferably material – possibly the body itself or nature – which is comforting because it is still there. Indulging the senses in some way often helps too, through food, sex or body care. So does taking charge of the practicalities of the immediate situation, even if this is only mixing the drinks or passing out clipboards. To feel secure, you need continuity and a sense that you have your hand on the rudder of your own life. Think of the rather irreverent joke about the man seeming to cross himself in a crisis, all the while actually touching his most valued possessions to check that they are still intact – spectacles, testicles, wallet and watch. That must have been thought up by someone with the Moon in an earth sign.

Air Moons

When your Moon is in an air sign – Gemini, Libra or Aquarius – you feel most secure when you can stand back from situations and observe them from a distance. Too much intimacy chokes you and you'll tend to escape it by going into your head to the safety of ideas and analysis. Even in close relationships you need your mental, and preferably physical, space. You often have to think, talk or write about what you are feeling before you are sure what your feelings are. By putting them 'out there' so that you can examine them clearly, you can claim them as your own. Unfairness and unethical behaviour can upset you badly and make you feel uneasy until you have done something about it or responded in some way. It can be easy with an air Moon to be unaware of, or to ignore, your own feelings because you are more responsive to ideas, people and situations outside of yourself that may seem to have little connection with you. This is not a good idea, as it cuts you off from the needs of your body as well as your own emotional intelligence. Making opportunities to talk, play with and exchange ideas and information can reduce the stress levels if anxiety strikes.

Water Moons

Finally, if your Moon is in a water sign – Cancer, Scorpio or Pisces – you are ultra-sensitive to atmospheres, and you can experience other people's pain or distress as if they were your own. You tend to take everything personally and, even if the situation has nothing at all to do with you, feel responsible for making it better. Your worst nightmare is to feel no emotional response coming back from other people. That activates your deep-seated terror of abandonment, which can make you feel that you don't exist and is, quite literally, what you fear even more than death. If you feel insecure, you may be tempted to resort to emotional manipulation to try to force intimacy with others – not a good idea, as this can lead to the very rejection that you dread. You are at your most secure when the emotional climate is positive and you have trusted, supportive folk around who will winkle you out of hiding if you become too reclusive. With a water Moon, it is vital to learn to value your own feelings and to take them seriously – and to have a safe, private place you can retreat to when you feel emotionally fragile. As you never forget anything which has made a feeling impression on you, sometimes your reactions are triggered by unconscious memories of things long past, rather than what is taking place in the present. When you learn to interpret them correctly, your feelings are your finest ally and will serve you well.

Finding Your Moon Sign

If you don't yet know your Moon sign, before looking it up, you could have some fun reading through the descriptions that follow and seeing if you can guess which one it is. To find your Moon sign, check your year and date of birth in the tables on pp.99–112. For a greater in-depth understanding of your Moon sign, you might like to read about its characteristics in the book in this series about that sign.

At the beginning of each section are the names of some well-known Sagittarians with that particular Moon sign. You can find more about them in Chapter Ten.

Sun in Sagittarius with Moon in Aries

John Brown	Ada Byron	Mark Twain
Connie Francis	Kiefer Sutherland	Archduke Franz Ferdinand

Your mission is to develop the courage to stick up for yourself, and have your own needs met, without steamrollering over the agendas of others. Many of those born between 1943 and 1956 may find that first part particularly difficult and prefer to avoid conflict, especially with their mothers or children, at all costs. Being independent to the core, as well as fiercely outspoken, it would be surprising if you haven't had some stormy run-ins with authority. Mark Twain criticised the police of San Francisco so severely that the officials found means of making the writer's life there difficult. Once he even had to leave town hastily because of a duel over an article. Likewise, there may, or may not, be anything in rumours that the relationship between Queen Victoria and her highland servant John Brown was more than a friendship, but he was familiar far beyond his rank, leading to battles royal with courtiers.

Hot-tempered, impulsive and bossy, you tend to live for the moment, throwing yourself passionately into all your projects. Even if you don't feel combative yourself, you can be sure you'll be embroiled in conflict somehow, though fortunately rarely as violently as in the case of Archduke Franz Ferdinand. His assassination led to the outbreak of the First World War. Being far-sighted, you are quick to grasp possibilities long before others – and you'll act on them.

You thrive on challenge, the tougher the better. You feel at your most comfortable when you've a new enterprise to spearhead. There's practically no holding you back once you've decided to do something – and you want to do it your way. Strenuous physical exercise could be just the thing to restore some calm if you've been cooped up too long.

Sun in Sagittarius with Moon in Taurus

Ronnie Corbett	Jean-Luc Godard	Jim Morrison
Pamela Stephenson	Joanna Trollope	Dionne Warwick

Your need for stability can mean that you may be a little more cautious, canny and sceptical than most Sagittarians. With your energy, drive and enterprise, coupled with dogged staying power and sound business instincts, you have what it takes to ground your vision and produce concrete and lasting results, as you can balance your love of taking a risk or gamble with down-to-earth common sense. Your challenge is to balance your impulse to create a comfortable, permanent base with your equally powerful need for adventure, enterprise and exploring truths that lie beyond the limited world of the senses. Although you do like change, when it happens too fast, especially on the domestic front, you can feel unsettled. You probably have strong ideas about how the world should be run and, given half a chance, you could develop into a bit of a control freak. It's worth checking from time to time that your views haven't become too deeply entrenched.

Security for you lies in the tangible things of life: owning your own home, preferably in the country, and a regular supply of good food and satisfying sex. Be careful, though, not to overindulge your bodily appetites. Jim Morrison of The Doors went way over the top in this, finally dying of a heroin overdose. You do know how to enjoy yourself; beauty, colour, music, drama and art, as well as nature, give you great pleasure. Any career where you can preach your own gospel – and earn a steady income – is perfect for you. If you feel under stress, an hour or two in the garden, getting in tune with the slow rhythms of nature, would do you the world of good.

Sun in Sagittarius with Moon in Gemini

Billy Connolly	Noël Coward	Hermione Gingold
Petra Kelly	Julianne Moore	Tina Turner

Incurably curious and sometimes downright nosy, you delight in every experience that life sends your way – and often seek out more. Wisecracking actress Hermione Gingold used to forage, unashamedly, in other people's dustbins for what she could find. You've a wonderful knack of making connections that few others notice, and finding ingenious solutions to intellectual or practical problems. The comedian Billy Connolly often focuses on tiny interesting details, savouring them like nectar and twisting them this way and that to extract the last drop of fun. With your needle-sharp responses, you too probably have a wonderful turn of phrase, as words fascinate you, and you love to play with them. You've a low boredom threshold and like to keep up-to-date with what is happening in your field. You've an instinct for spotting upcoming trends, as did Petra Kelly, who founded the Green Party, and bringing them to the world's attention.

Running on so much nervous energy, it's hard for you to know when enough is enough, and to take a break. Your challenge is to keep in touch with what's fresh around you, yet tune in to your own needs, too, flipping your attention backwards and forwards between the messages that bombard you from inside and outside – and not to get distracted by whatever seems most interesting. Part of you will never grow up. Settling down in just one place isn't easy. Many with Gemini Moons have had a childhood punctuated by several home moves and you may, as an adult, prefer to have two or more places you can call your home. Communicating is as essential to you as breathing, so having a partner with whom you can swap ideas is vital.

Sun in Sagittarius with Moon in Cancer

Sai Baba	William Blake	Edith Cavell
Jimi Hendrix	Pat Phoenix	Donny Osmond

Beneath that freewheeling exterior, you're more sensitive, and possibly timid, than you care to admit, even to yourself. Being highly intuitive, you quickly tune in to the feelings and needs of those around you. This can give you the common touch and an excellent rapport with others – a great advantage if you work with the public. You tend to be gentle, kind and helpful to those who are vulnerable. You are easily moved to tears by any strong sentiment, and your feelings can sometimes get the better of you. It's not always easy for you to understand your own moods. You may be touchy and irritable at times, and interpret other people's withdrawals and sulks as a personal snub when, in reality, they may have nothing at all to do with you. Being terrified of humiliation and rejection, you could act cynically as self-protection.

It's important for you to find, or create, a cosy, protective nest where you can retreat from the world, even if it's only inside your head. You need the safety net of emotional, financial and domestic security and comfort to fall back on, or you can become quite ungrounded. Your support network is crucial to you – either blood relatives or chosen intimates whom you'll regard as family. The Moon in Cancer can be clannish and focused on its own backyard, while the Sun in Sagittarius craves adventure and foreignness. Your challenge is to integrate both. Nurse Edith Cavell, a war heroine, realised this. In her last letter, before being executed by the Germans for saving Allied soldiers, she wrote the words that are chiselled on her monument in London: 'Patriotism is not enough, I must have no hatred or bitterness towards anyone.'

Sun in Sagittarius with Moon in Leo

| Winston Churchill | Martin Clunes | Benjamin Disraeli |
| Jane Fonda | Christina Rossetti | Nancy Mitford |

Your instinct, in any situation, is to move into centre-stage and take on a leadership and advisory role. When all eyes are on you, looking up to you expectantly for words of wisdom and guidance, you really come into your own. There is no way you are going to be overlooked – or allow yourself to be. Being ignored or treated as insignificant can make you feel out of sorts and grumpy, so it's vital that you find some place in your life where it is appropriate for you to shine and be admired. As you need to feel special, and hate to be looked down on, you do tend to act honourably if you feel you're in the spotlight – unless you take on the role of villain, in which case you'll be an arch-villain.

Unfortunately, once you have a project you want to promote, you may have a tendency to trample all over other people's sensitivities and agendas without the slightest idea that you're doing so. When the chips are down, your sterling qualities surface. Being charismatic and a natural commander, you'll rally your forces and come up trumps. You are an inspiration to others, encouraging them to give of their best as Winston Churchill did in the Second World War, with his magnificent oratory, which inspired and sustained the British people through their darkest hours. If your dignity is ruffled, or things aren't going exactly your way, the world may be treated to a pyrotechnics display. You can be generous to a fault, if a bit imperious. Churchill said in his diaries that he did not suffer from any desire to be relieved of his responsibilities. All he wanted was compliance with his wishes, after reasonable discussion. And that just about sums you up, too.

Sun in Sagittarius with Moon in Virgo

| Kenneth Branagh | Maria Callas | Thomas Carlyle |
| Sammy Davis Jr | Dorothy Lamour | Frank Zappa |

Sloppiness, especially in thinking, can drive you to distraction. With your ability to spot a flaw a mile off, you've a highly critical mind, and often a tongue to match. The historian and sage Thomas Carlyle is reported to have been 'churlish and uncharitable to the work and personalities of others'. You can be just as critical of yourself as you are of others, sometimes even more so.

A well-crafted task gives you immense satisfaction and you'll go to endless trouble to sort out the details and to do it properly. Theories rarely interest you unless they lead to useful results. Practical action is what appeals. You may have to be careful not to become a workaholic and lose out on a lot of life's fun. Frank Zappa, the moustachioed rock star, said that he wasn't a tourist and didn't take vacations – the only reason he left home was to work. Without labour that you love, and someone or something to serve, or to improve, you can feel incomplete. There is part of you that is quite immune to current trends or fashions. To feel good about yourself, you need to go deep inside and identify what you sense is right and then act on that sense of rightness, no matter what everyone else is saying or doing. To go against this quiet voice is to betray your own integrity. You like to do things with precision and orderly rituals, even simple ones, can be immensely comforting in times of stress. You may have an interest in healthy living. If so, there won't be many around you who haven't heard a sermon or two preached on the subject.

Sun in Sagittarius with Moon in Libra

Jane Austen	Emily Dickinson	Walt Disney
Charles I	Françoise Gilot	Henri de Toulouse-Lautrec

You're such an idealist that you may find the real world hard to take. Most won't, however, go to the lengths of the American poet Emily Dickinson, who withdrew completely into the solitude of an ivory tower or Walt Disney, who created his own airbrushed fantasia, then sold it to the world for a healthy profit. Coming up against the darker side of human nature can be a nasty shock because it's often difficult for you to grasp the fact that some people are just not as principled as you believe you are. As you've a well-developed sense of justice and the ability to see everybody's viewpoint, you may have a keen interest in political issues. Unfairness upsets you and you'll put your considerable energies into redressing the balance. If you feel that you've caused offence or that people don't like you, you'll be on edge until the situation has been righted. Relationship is of the utmost importance to you and you'll find it hard not to have someone around, if only to bounce ideas off. You love to debate, sometimes shifting sides mid-flow if you feel another part of the argument is under-represented.

You are an excellent strategic planner and have a knack of getting people on your side through charm and diplomacy. Women with Libra Moons often have a steeliness of resolve under a charming exterior, and refuse to stay put in a 'woman's role', while men can have an instinctive empathy with women, and may prefer their company to that of other men. Grace and graciousness come easily to you – give or take a temper tantrum or two – and a home filled with light, art and beauty is food for your soul.

Sun in Sagittarius with Moon in Scorpio

King George VI	J. Paul Getty	Bruce Lee
Bette Midler	Edna O'Brien	Steven Spielberg

You tend to be secretive about your true feelings, revealing them only when you are absolutely sure you can trust your confidant, or never at all. Many with this combination have had experiences of bullying as a child, as did the Queen's father King George VI, who ended up with a nervous stutter.

You may find it hard to trust and, if you have been hurt, may be tempted to hurt others yourself. Your greatest challenge is to refuse to be a victim and use your formidable willpower, insight and honesty to drop resentments, which you tend to brood over, and create a better future for everyone, including yourself. When you feel safe, you can be kind, tender, loyal and affectionate. If your trust is then betrayed, you'll cut that person dead for ever more – or worse.

Sex, secrets, money and power can fascinate you and it's likely that these will be dominant themes in your life. Uninhibited comedienne Bette Midler started her steamy career in a gay men's bath club. Steven Spielberg confronts death, danger and darkness in his films which, like *Schindler's List* and *Jurassic Park*, often have strong moral messages. This is a wonderful combination for making money, bringing together as it does the Sagittarian love of thinking big, taking a risk and trusting your hunches, with the Scorpionic instinctive tingling of the flesh whenever money and power are near at hand. You have a deep reserve of emotional strength that comes to your aid when your back is to the wall. You may surprise even yourself with how resourceful a survivor you are, and how feeling under threat can bring out the best, or worst, in you.

Sun in Sagittarius with Moon in Sagittarius

Joan Armatrading	Jacques Chirac	Alicia Markova
Humphrey Davy	'Lucky' Luciano	General George Custer

You like nothing better than taking a risk and you'll push your luck to the limit, hoping that you'll get away with it, and so often you do. General Custer had 19 horses shot from under him before his luck finally ran out in his last stand at Little Bighorn. Even if life does hand you a lemon, with your eye for opportunities, you'll make lemonade and manage to market it as the finest champagne. 'Lucky' Luciano was a New York mobster boss and entrepreneur who made a fortune from prostitution, smuggling and racketeering. His nickname came from his surviving an assassination attempt early in his career. He was sent to prison in 1936 for 50 years, but was released in 1946 for helping the Allies to land forces in Sicily by securing local cooperation through his powerful connections. He also helped tighten security on New York's dockland – all of this achieved from a prison cell. You're unlikely to be a mobster but, like Luciano, you're almost certainly an eternal optimist and, whatever the circumstances, will manage to come out from under, smiling and in profit.

A born rover and entertainer, in love with the adventure of life, you're constantly in search of a widening horizon – and you need to move your body. The ballerina Alicia Markova developed her muscles and technique to such an extent that she gave the appearance of flying. You need a partner who can share your enthusiasms and will give you plenty of freedom – General Custer's wife accompanied him to the battlefront. Generous to a fault, unless stingier chart factors are present, you probably love splashing the cash around and it could be a case with you of easy come, easy go.

Sun in Sagittarius with Moon in Capricorn

| Kim Basinger | Jane Birkin | Charles Forte |
| Mary, Queen of Scots | Edvard Munch | Christina Onassis |

You feel most comfortable and secure when you have an official title or a place of standing in the community, but you may not go as far as Kim Basinger, who bought up a whole town in her home state of Georgia. Community standing doesn't come much bigger than that. Given half a chance, you could be excellent in business, combining Capricorn caution and prudent judgement with your ability to spot an opportunity and love of taking a risk. Christina Onassis, daughter of the shipping magnate Aristotle Onassis, was considered a natural in the commercial world and managed, more than competently, the millions of dollars that flowed through her business daily.

You may have had to grow up fast. Many with this combination have come from humble backgrounds, have known tragedy in early life or were raised in homes where correct behaviour and discipline were the rule, rather than spontaneity and warm acceptance. The inspiration for much of the work of Edvard Munch, painter of *The Scream*, was his early memories of illness, death and grief. Few, though, have borne such heavy responsibilities and so much tragedy with as much nobility as Mary, who, on the death of her father, became Queen of Scotland only six days after she was born – and that was only the start of her journey. Hard work is as familiar to you as breathing, and if you put your considerable energy into achieving your goals, it will almost guarantee that you acquire the status, recognition and respect you crave. Just be careful, though, not to neglect your home life in the process. It takes time to create a happy home, but if anyone can do it, you can.

Sun in Sagittarius with Moon in Aquarius

Woody Allen	Louisa M. Alcott	Andrew Carnegie
Margaret Mead	Britney Spears	Marie Tussaud

Louisa M. Alcott defined a philosopher as a man up in a

balloon, with his family and friends holding the ropes which confine him to earth, and trying to pull him down. This could well describe you, too. An Aquarius Moon often prefers to stay above all the petty affairs of everyday life. It's not that you feel that you are higher, mightier and better than others; it's actually quite the reverse. You are often so caught up with the concerns of the whole wide world that you can forget your own emotional and physical needs, and ignore what's right under your nose at home.

You could be a philanthropist and humanitarian, like the business tycoon Andrew Carnegie. He decided that he would spend the first part of his life making a lot of money and the second half giving it away, and that's exactly what he did. He spent most of it on libraries, trust funds and educational facilities to give ordinary people opportunities. His motto on the coat of arms he devised for himself was 'Death to Privilege'.

You like things logical and clear-cut, yet your moods can be quite contrary. One moment you may be abrupt and withdrawn, but you'll be chatty and friendly the next. Others may see you as aloof and even a bit of an oddball or loner. You are much more at ease with friendships than intimacy, and if anybody tries to get too close, you'll feel choked. Your home is likely to be unconventional in some way and you may find it hard to put down roots, emotional or geographical, anywhere. For contentment, you need to find some way of opening and widening your family circle to let in the wider world.

Sun in Sagittarius with Moon in Pisces

Charles Schultz	Curt Jurgens	Frank Sinatra
Frances Hodgson Burnett	Gianni Versace	Bill Wilson

Beneath that happy-go-lucky exterior you may feel chronically insecure and not quite at home on this planet. You tend to shrink away from harshness of any kind and may much prefer to be reclusive. Fortunately, though, you are unlikely to have the extreme sensitivity of Charles M. Schultz, creator of Peanuts, who, despite outstanding success, lived with overwhelming feelings of worthlessness and anxiety. It was he who coined the phrase 'security blanket' and that's exactly what you would like to keep wrapped round you at all times. You are so acutely aware of any suffering around you that you often pick up other people's feelings and experience them as if they were your own. You can feel guilty and responsible for putting right the woes of the world. Frank Sinatra once rescued a hurt dog and insisted on taking it to the vet himself, despite the fact that he was on his way to an important business meeting.

Frequent escapes from everyday reality are essential for your well-being, preferably not through alcohol or drugs, as this can get out of hand. To help others, Bill Wilson, founder of Alcoholics Anonymous, wrote *The Twelve Steps and Twelve Traditions*, now the standard text for many programmes of recovery from a wide variety of addictions. Frances Hodgson Burnett penned the children's classic *The Secret Garden*, which is a beautiful Pisces Moon escapist fantasy. As a child, you probably felt responsible for looking after others, especially your mother, and learned to read emotional atmospheres in order to have your own needs met indirectly. Public figures with Pisces Moons can pick up on instantly, and provide, the fantasy their audience longs for, and so capture their imagination to great advantage.

EIGHT

Mercury – It's All in the Mind

THE GLYPHS FOR THE PLANETS ARE MADE UP OF THREE SYMBOLS: the circle, the semi-circle and the cross. Mercury is the only planet, apart from Pluto, whose glyph is made up of all three of these symbols. At the bottom there is the cross, representing the material world; at the top is the semi-circle of the crescent Moon, symbolising the personal soul; and in the middle, linking these two, is the circle of eternity, expressed through the individual. In mythology, Mercury was the only god who had access to all three worlds – the underworld, the middle world of earth and the higher world of the gods. Mercury in your chart represents your ability, through your thoughts and words, to make connections between the inner world of your mind and emotions, the outer world of other people and events, and the higher world of intuition. Your Mercury sign can give you a great deal of information about the way your mind works and about your interests, communication skills and your preferred learning style.

It can be frustrating when we just can't get through to some people and it's easy to dismiss them as being either completely thick or deliberately obstructive. Chances are they are neither. It may be that you're simply not talking each other's languages. Knowing your own and other people's communication styles can lead to major breakthroughs in relationships.

Information about children's natural learning patterns can help us teach them more effectively. It's impossible to learn properly if the material isn't presented in a way that resonates with the way your mind works. You just can't 'hear' it, pick it up or grasp it. Wires then get crossed and the data simply isn't processed. Many children are seriously disadvantaged if learning materials and environments don't speak to them. You may even have been a child like that yourself. If so, you could easily have been left with the false impression that you are a poor learner just because you couldn't get a handle on the lessons being taught. Identifying your own learning style can be like finding the hidden key to the treasure room of knowledge.

The signs of the zodiac are divided into four groups by element:

> The fire signs: Aries, Leo and Sagittarius
> The earth signs: Taurus, Virgo and Capricorn
> The air signs: Gemini, Libra and Aquarius
> The water signs: Cancer, Scorpio and Pisces

Your Mercury will therefore belong to one of the four elements, depending on which sign it is in. Your Mercury can only be in one of three signs – the same sign as your Sun, the one before or the one after. This means that each sign has one learning style that is never natural to it. For Sagittarius, this is the air style.

Mercury in each of the elements has a distinctive way of

operating. I've given the following names to the learning and communicating styles of Mercury through the elements. Mercury in fire – active imaginative; Mercury in earth – practical; Mercury in air – logical; and Mercury in water – impressionable.

Mercury in Fire: Active Imaginative

Your mind is wide open to the excitement of fresh ideas. It responds to action and to the creative possibilities of new situations. Drama, games and storytelling are excellent ways for you to learn. You love to have fun and play with ideas. Any material to be learned has to have some significance for you personally, or add to your self-esteem, otherwise you rapidly lose interest. You learn by acting out the new information, either physically or in your imagination. The most efficient way of succeeding in any goal is to make first a mental picture of your having achieved it. This is called mental rehearsal and is used by many top sportsmen and women as a technique to help improve their performance. You do this spontaneously, as your imagination is your greatest mental asset. You can run through future scenarios in your mind's eye and see, instantly, where a particular piece of information or situation could lead and spot possibilities that other people couldn't even begin to dream of. You are brilliant at coming up with flashes of inspiration for creative breakthroughs and crisis management.

Mercury in Earth: Practical

Endless presentations of feelings, theories and possibilities can make your eyes glaze over and your brain ache to shut down. What really turns you on is trying out these theories and possibilities to see if they work in practice. If they don't, you'll tend to classify them 'of no further interest'. Emotionally charged information is at best a puzzling non-starter and at worst an irritating turn-off. Practical demonstrations, tried and tested facts and working models fascinate you. Hands-on learning, where you can see how a process functions from start to finish, especially if it leads to some useful material end-product, is right up your street. It's important to allow yourself plenty of time when you are learning, writing or thinking out what to say, otherwise you can feel rushed and out of control, never pleasant sensations for earth signs. Your special skill is in coming up with effective solutions to practical problems and in formulating long-range plans that bring concrete, measurable results.

Mercury in Air: Logical

You love learning about, and playing with, ideas, theories and principles. Often you do this best by arguing or bouncing ideas off other people, or by writing down your thoughts. Your special gift is in your ability to stand back and work out the patterns of relationship between people or things. You much prefer it when facts are presented to you logically and unemotionally and have very little time for the irrational, uncertainty or for personal opinions. You do, though, tend to have plenty of those kinds of views yourself, only you call them logical conclusions. Whether a fact is useful or not is less important than whether it fits into your mental map of how the world operates. If facts don't fit in, you'll either ignore them, find a way of making them fit, or, occasionally, make a grand leap to a new, upgraded theory. Yours is the mind of the scientist or chess player. You make a brilliant planner because you can be detached enough to take an overview of the entire situation.

Mercury in Water: Impressionable

Your mind is sensitive to atmospheres and emotional undertones and to the context in which information is presented. Plain facts and figures can often leave you cold and even intimidated. You can take things too personally and read between the lines for what you believe is really being said or taught. If you don't feel emotionally safe, you can be cautious about revealing your true thoughts. It may be hard, or even impossible, for you to learn properly in what you sense is a hostile environment. You are excellent at impression management. Like a skilful artist painting a picture, you can influence others to think what you'd like them to by using suggestive gestures or pauses and intonations. People with Mercury in water signs are often seriously disadvantaged by left-brain schooling methods that are too rigidly structured for them. You take in information best through pictures or images, so that you get a 'feel' for the material and can make an emotional bond with it, in the same way you connect with people. In emotionally supportive situations where there is a rapport between you and your instructors, or your learning material, you are able just to drink in and absorb circulating knowledge without conscious effort, sometimes not even being clear about how or why you know certain things.

Finding Your Mercury Sign

If you don't yet know your Mercury sign, you might like to see if you can guess what it is from the descriptions below before checking it out in the tables on pp.113–15.

Sun in Sagittarius with Mercury in Scorpio

William Blake	Andrew Carnegie	Winston Churchill
Billy Connolly	Sinead O'Connor	Mark Twain

It's hard to fool you, as your mind works like a ferret down a rabbit-hole, burrowing beneath the surface to discover what is really going on. You can spot cover-ups, scams and hypocrisy insantly and probably take great delight in exposing them, too. Comedian Billy Connolly is merciless about unravelling human motivations and laying bare the mysteries of bodily functions that few others would dream of examining. The mystic poet William Blake was also a taboo-breaker, especially when he and his wife insisted on being married in 1782 in the full glory of their birthday suits. He was also tried, and acquitted, for uttering 'treasonable expressions'.

Anyone who offends you is likely to receive, by return, a poisoned verbal dart laced with wit. Churchill came back quick as a flash to fellow politician Nancy Astor, when she told him that if she were his wife she would put poison in his coffee. He replied that if he were her husband, he would drink it. It's probably better to retaliate immediately, as you have a tendency to hold grudges, and resentment does your health and temper no good.

No matter how friendly you seem, you'll usually prefer to keep your thoughts private and to guard your privacy firmly. You may, or may not, have anything to hide, but that's nobody's business but your own. Money, sex, power and the meaning of life and the secrets of death are rarely far from your thoughts. Your mind works in a cyclical way, sometimes brilliantly articulate, at other times seeming to have nothing to offer to the outside world. Then is the time for stocking up on your inner mental resources through reading and reflection.

Sun in Sagittarius with Mercury in Sagittarius

Emily Dickinson	Uri Geller	Bette Midler
Pat Phoenix	Steven Spielberg	Tina Turner

You paint your life on a large canvas and, above all, you think big. Even if you live in restricted circumstances, your mind will find a way to soar unrestrained. The poet Emily Dickinson spent her whole life secluded in her family home, writing what have been considered some of the finest American poems ever. Her travels were in the imagination. As she wrote, 'There is no Frigate like a Book, to take us Lands away.'

No matter how many difficulties life scatters in your way, your thoughts have the power to disperse gloom like the wave of a magic wand. You may not be able to bend spoons as well as Uri Geller but, if you can learn to focus and direct them, your thoughts and beliefs can work other miracles. Mercury in Sagittarius gives generosity of mind and spirit and a genius for inspiring those around you to do the seemingly impossible and make the most of their potential. Even if you have little formal education, with your thirst for knowledge, you are likely to be very well-informed indeed. You may, however, also have a double helping of Sagittarian tactlessness, which can wound other people's sensitivities simply by telling the unvarnished truth. Because of your optimism and faith that it will all work out somehow, you have little fear of taking on big projects, but you may need to make sure that you don't promise, in the heat of the moment, more than you can deliver when your enthusiasm has died down. With your unquenchable belief in the human spirit to rise above rank and race, you are an internationalist and democrat at heart.

Sun in Sagittarius with Mercury in Capricorn

Joan Armatrading	Benjamin Disraeli	Gordon Jackson
Mary, Queen of Scots	Brad Pitt	Joanna Trollope

Some people may find you a little formal or reserved, and even slightly frosty in the way you communicate, and you've probably been told from time to time that you've an old head on your shoulders. You like to ponder well before saying anything important. While you may not always be a spontaneous communicator, once you get started it's as if an icecap has melted and your words flow freely and fluently.

You could be inclined to calculation and making long-term arrangements, even down to sorting out your pension from an early age. At the back of your mind, there's often a master plan for climbing up the ladder of success, whatever that means for you. While you may not be an intellectual, recognition for some kind of mental contribution would bring you immense satisfaction, but you may be a little shy or nervous about how your words will be received. You have a practical mind and probably welcome a formal or traditional approach to learning and may even take a responsible attitude towards helping others learn, as Capricorn is the sign of the community elder. Brad Pitt has donated $100,000 to a children's learning museum in his home town.

You like to feel in control, especially in business deals

and contracts, and though it may be a bore, you're inclined to read the small print carefully. As you are not always, like most Sagittarians, inclined to look on the bright side of life, you may be prone to gloomy thoughts or even the occasional depression. This can frequently prove constructive; weighing up your doubts and fears against reality and possibilities will help you make some shrewd choices.

NINE

Venus – At Your Pleasure

♀ THE GLYPH FOR VENUS IS MADE UP OF THE CIRCLE OF ETERNITY on top of the cross of matter. Esoterically this represents love, which is a quality of the divine, revealed on earth through personal choice. The saying 'One man's meat is another man's poison' couldn't be more relevant when it comes to what we love. It is a mystery why we find one thing attractive and another unattractive, or even repulsive. Looking at the sign, aspects and house of your Venus can't give any explanation of this mystery, but it can give some clear indications of what it is that you value and find desirable. This can be quite different from what current fashion tells you you should like. For example, many people are strongly turned on by voluptuous bodies but the media constantly shows images of near-anorexics as the desirable ideal. If you ignore what you, personally, find beautiful and try to be, or to love, what at heart leaves you cold, you are setting yourself up for unnecessary pain and dissatisfaction. Being true to your Venus sign, even if other people think you are strange, brings joy and pleasure. It also builds up your self-esteem because it grounds you solidly in your own personal values. This, in turn, makes you much more attractive to others. Not only that, it improves your relationships immeasurably, because you are living authentically and not betraying yourself by trying to prove your worth to others by being something you are not.

Glittering Venus, the brightest planet in the heavens, was named after the goddess of love, war and victory. Earlier names for her were Aphrodite, Innana and Ishtar. She was beautiful, self-willed and self-indulgent but was also skilled in all the arts of civilisation.

Your Venus sign shows what you desire and would like to possess, not only in relationships but also in all aspects of your taste, from clothes and culture to hobbies and hobby-horses. It identifies how and where you can be charming and seductive and skilful at creating your own type of beauty yourself. It also describes your style of attracting partners and the kind of people that turn you on. When your Venus is activated you feel powerful, desirable and wonderfully, wickedly indulged and indulgent. When it is not, even if someone has all the right credentials to make a good match, the relationship will always lack that certain something. If you don't take the chance to express your Venus to a good enough degree somewhere in your life, you miss out woefully on delight and happiness.

Morning Star, Evening Star

Venus appears in the sky either in the morning or in the evening. The ancients launched their attacks when Venus became a morning star, believing that she was then in her warrior-goddess role, releasing aggressive energy for victory in battle. If you're a morning-star person, you're likely to be impulsive, self-willed and idealistic, prepared to hold out until you find the partner who is just right for you.

Relationships and business dealings of morning-star Venus people are said to prosper best whenever Venus in the sky is a morning star. If you are an early bird, you can check this out. At these times Venus can be seen in the eastern sky before the Sun has risen.

The name for Venus as an evening star is Hesperus and it was then, traditionally, said to be sacred to lovers. Evening-star people tend to be easy-going and are open to negotiation, conciliation and making peace. If you are an evening-star Venus person, your best times in relationship and business affairs are said to be when Venus can be seen, jewel-like, in the western sky after the Sun has set.

Because the orbit of Venus is so close to the Sun, your Venus can only be in one of five signs. You have a morning-star Venus if your Venus is in one of the two signs that come before your Sun sign in the zodiac. You have an evening-star Venus if your Venus is in either of the two signs that follow your Sun sign. If you have Venus in the same sign as your Sun, you could be either, depending on whether your Venus is ahead of or behind your Sun. (You can find out which at the author's website www.janeridderpatrick.com.)

If you don't yet know your Venus sign, you might like to read through all of the following descriptions and see if you can guess what it is. You can find out for sure on pp.116–18.

At the beginning of each section are the names of some well-known Sagittarians with that particular Venus sign. You can find out more about them in Chapter Ten, Famous Sagittarius Birthdays.

Sun in Sagittarius with Venus in Libra

| Woody Allen | Bill Wilson | Friedrich Engels |
| Charles Forte | Anna Freud | Andy Williams |

Harmony in marriage and all social relationships mean a lot to you but there can be a conflict between your strong desire for partnership and an equally powerful craving for freedom. You may have to work at finding some kind of compromise because you need both in your life. You can be a little naive and idealistic about relationships, expecting that, once matters have been formalised, you will gallop into the sunset where undiluted contentment awaits you forever after. Even if, like Woody Allen, you're not classically good-looking, you'll exude an air of attractiveness. You'd prefer your partner to be well-groomed, intelligent and easy on the eye, too. When it comes to romance, you're a stylish lover and like the full works – flowers, candlelit dinners, flirtation . . . 'Moon River', sung by Andy Williams, is surely one of the most romantic love songs ever, and just about sums up your view of love.

As you dislike open confrontation, you are apt to be over-tolerant in situations where it might be better to nip the problem in the bud, instead of hoping that all will be well if you are nice to everybody. It can be difficult for you to untangle from relationships, as you dislike un-pleasantness, so if you've had enough you could misbehave or just withdraw, easing the way for your partner to be the one to leave you. Nothing, however, upsets you more than injustice and unfairness and you'll go to great lengths to put the balance right, even if you have to ruffle a few feathers in the process. You enjoy debating, can put your own case across skilfully and may even, like Engels, who co-wrote *The Communist Manifesto*, be drawn to supporting political causes.

Sagittarius Sun with Venus in Scorpio

Jane Austen	Edith Cavell	Lucien Freud
William Hogarth	Edna O'Brien	Steven Spielberg

Venus in Scorpio adds depth and intensity to the freewheeling optimism of your Sagittarian Sun. Skimming over the surface of life will never fully satisfy you. You want to prise off polite facades to discover what's underneath. Secrets and mysteries intrigue you, and you may have a fascination, possibly tinged with fear or foreboding, about the darker, or forbidden, sides of life, like sex and death and power struggles for survival. You can be a formidable researcher, as once you've sunk your teeth into a puzzle you'll never let go until you find an answer. You are not afraid of looking truth in the eye, even if it is uncomfortable. The paintings of Lucian Freud treat the bodies of his subjects in an almost shockingly unsentimental fashion, yet reveal a tough truth about human mortality. In a similar way, William Hogarth's pictures, like *A Rake's Progress*, are unvarnished social commentaries on the decadence of the eighteenth-century London slums.

Coupling your interest, and understanding, of the dynamics of power – physical, emotional or spiritual – with an eye for the main chance can give you a knack of turning life's dross into diamonds, which could allow you to make money from what society rejects.

Venus in Scorpio can mean a powerful sex drive and, like

everything else in Scorpio, it can go to extremes, prompting you to be uncompromisingly faithful, or to take every opportunity to indulge your appetites, which may be off the beaten track and even rather taboo. Alternatively, you could direct most of that intense energy into your life's work. You may be drawn to partners who are powerful, either in personality or position, or who ooze subtle but unmistakable sexuality, as you do yourself.

Sun in Sagittarius with Venus in Sagittarius

Sai Baba	Andrew Carnegie	Winston Churchill
Emily Dickinson	Jane Fonda	Sinead O'Connor

Almost every Sagittarius loves to preach and uplift, but you have elevated those to an art form. Winston Churchill's wartime speeches are oratory at its inspiring best. Even after more than half a century, his words still have the power to stir. Unless you have a mission, and a vision to spread, you will not feel fully content. Not that your beliefs and causes always stay the same. Sinead O'Connor once caused uproar after she tore up a picture of the Pope, shouting 'Fight the true evil.' She later became reconciled with the church and was ordained as a priest. Similarly, Jane Fonda became a passionate opponent of the Vietnam War but later apologised for the harm she had done by lowering morale. Like them, your view of the world shifts and enlarges, and you'll want to keep that same world updated on your current passionate stance.

You make an inspiring teacher and, with your magical gift of optimism and faith, leave the lives of those you have touched the better for your having passed through them. Tact, however, may not be your forte; nor, indeed, fidelity.

You may choose partners who are foreigners or connected with publishing, travel, the law or religion. Relationships where you learn from, or teach, others help you develop wisdom and little stirs you up as much as discussing the meaning of life, and your own part in it. It would be hard for you to stay committed to a partner who did not either share your beliefs and passionate causes or, at least, allow you plenty of freedom to pursue these interests alone. You hate to be stuck in one place, physically or mentally, and travelling, exploring new ideas and even risk and danger will keep your spirits up.

Sun in Sagittarius with Venus in Capricorn

| Louisa M. Alcott | John Brown | Maria Callas |
| Dale Carnegie | John Milton | Britney Spears |

When it comes to long-term relationships, you may not be the most romantic creature on the planet, as you are rather formal and take it all so very seriously. Any commitment you make, you want to last, and you can spend a considerable time making up your mind before tying the knot. The advantage is that you'll tend to go into contracts with your eyes wide open, unlike most other Sagittarians, so any partnership, either business or romantic, has a good chance of lasting. Tradition matters to you and so does doing the right thing. Louisa M. Alcott's popular books, *Little Women* and *Good Wives*, are both entertaining and an education in manners and social niceties at the same time. Dale Carnegie's classic *How to Win Friends and Influence People* spells out the businesslike rules of successful relating.

You may be drawn to partners who are much younger or

older – Maria Callas's first husband was 32 years her senior – or who are of a different station in life to you. Queen Victoria formed such a close attachment to her Highland servant John Brown that she was often referred to as Mrs Brown. You may, despite making the right choice, find that relationships bring with them heavy responsibilities or restrictions and it will depend on your maturity whether you cope well with this or not. As your career and standing in the community is important, you may have to be careful not to become a workaholic or miss out on fun – though that may well suit you. The poet John Milton wrote twin poems, *L'Allegro* and *Il Penseroso*, about the relative merits of fun and melancholy. On balance, he preferred the more sober of the two . . .

Sun in Sagittarius with Venus in Aquarius

| Kenneth Branagh | Arthur C. Clarke | Donny Osmond |
| Brenda Lee | Don Johnson | Margaret Mead |

While you love humanity as an abstract concept, you're not always so enamoured of individual people, especially when they get up close and personal. To have a commitment that lasts, a like-minded partner who shares your ideas and ideals is essential and you're happiest with a partner who is also your best mate. Too much togetherness and powerful emotions, especially of the dark and dangerous kind, can make you run for cover. Your natural emotional reserve can sometimes be mistaken for aloofness, but you are far from cold. You need the freedom to be chummy with just about everyone you meet, without the ball and chain of jealousy or disapproval following you around. Some Sagittarians with Venus in Aquarius are emotionally detached when it comes to sex, notching up conquests on the bedposts, their hearts untouched. Others, once committed, are so highly principled that they would almost rather die than deceive.

There is likely to be something quite unconventional about your interests, tastes or relationships. Apparently, Don Johnson seduced his babysitter when he was 12 and moved in with a woman of 25 when he was only 16. Being and staying at the cutting edge of your profession could bring you lasting happiness and satisfaction. You are likely to be skilled at networking, and even if you never see people you care for from one end of a decade to the other, or they live at the opposite side of the world, you will still feel connected. It is the meeting of minds that matters, not their presence in the same room. Friendship means a great deal to you and you can be endlessly generous to those you feel connected to through shared interests and beliefs.

TEN

Famous Sagittarius Birthdays

FIND OUT WHO SHARES YOUR MOON, MERCURY AND VENUS SIGNS AND ANY challenging Sun aspects and see what they have done with the material they were born with. Notice how often it is not just the personalities of the people themselves but the roles of actors, characters of authors and works of artists that reflect their astrological make-up. In reading standard biographies, I've been constantly astounded – and, of course, delighted – at how often phrases used to describe individuals could have been lifted straight from their astrological profiles. Check it out yourself!

A few people below have been given a choice of two Moons. This is because the Moon changed sign on the day that they were born and no birth time was available. You may be able to guess which one is correct if you read the descriptions of the Moon signs in Chapter Seven.

22 November
1932 Robert Vaughn, TV actor, *The Protectors*, *The Man From U.N.C.L.E.*
Sun aspects: Neptune
Moon: Virgo   Mercury: Sagittarius   Venus: Libra

23 November
1926 Sai Baba, controversial Indian guru who manifested objects from thin air
Sun aspects: Saturn, Neptune
Moon: Cancer   Mercury: Sagittarius   Venus: Sagittarius

24 November
1942 Billy Connolly, Scottish comedian and actor, *Mrs Brown*
Sun aspects: Saturn, Uranus
Moon: Gemini   Mercury: Scorpio   Venus: Sagittarius

25 November
1835 Andrew Carnegie, industrialist who donated millions and built Skibo Castle
Sun aspects: Uranus
Moon: Aquarius   Mercury: Scorpio   Venus: Sagittarius

26 November
1922 Charles M. Schultz, cartoonist and creator of *Peanuts*
Sun aspects: Uranus
Moon: Pisces   Mercury: Scorpio   Venus: Sagittarius

27 November
1940 Bruce Lee, martial arts star who died in mysterious circumstances
Sun aspects: none
Moon: Scorpio   Mercury: Scorpio   Venus: Scorpio

28 November
1757 William Blake, poet, artist and mystic, 'The Tyger'
Sun aspects: none
Moon: Cancer   Mercury: Scorpio   Venus: Capricorn

29 November
1832 Louisa M. Alcott, author, *Little Women, Good Wives*
Sun aspects: none
Moon: Aquarius   Mercury: Sagittarius   Venus: Capricorn

30 November
1874 Winston Churchill, British prime minister, orator and
inspiring leader in the Second World War
Sun aspects: none
Moon: Leo   Mercury: Scorpio   Venus: Sagittarius

1 December
1761 Marie Tussaud, creator of the waxworks museum in
London
Sun aspects: none
Moon: Aquarius   Mercury: Sagittarius   Venus: Scorpio

2 December
1923 Maria Callas, opera diva and lover of Aristotle Onassis
Sun aspects: Uranus
Moon: Virgo   Mercury: Sagittarius   Venus: Capricorn

3 December
1895 Anna Freud, founder of child psychoanalysis,
daughter of Sigmund Freud
Sun aspects: Neptune, Pluto
Moon: Gemini   Mercury: Sagittarius   Venus: Libra

4 December
1865 Edith Cavell, First World War nurse, shot for helping wounded British soldiers escape
Sun aspects: none
Moon: Cancer   Mercury: Capricorn   Venus: Scorpio

5 December
1901 Walt Disney, film-maker, creator of Mickey Mouse and Disneyland
Sun aspects: Uranus, Pluto
Moon: Libra   Mercury: Scorpio   Venus: Capricorn

6 December
1920 Dave Brubeck, jazz musician, 'Take Five'
Sun aspects: Saturn
Moon: Scorpio   Mercury: Scorpio   Venus: Capricorn

7 December
1928 Noam Chomsky, linguist and political activist, *The Political Economy of Human Rights*
Sun aspects: Saturn
Moon: Libra/Scorpio   Mercury: Sagittarius
Venus: Capricorn

8 December
1542 Mary, Queen of Scots
Sun aspects: none
Moon: Capricorn   Mercury: Capricorn   Venus: Sagittarius

9 December
1934 Judi Dench, actress, *Mrs Brown*, *Tea with Mussolini*
Sun aspects: Neptune
Moon: Capricorn   Mercury: Sagittarius   Venus: Sagittarius

10 December
1960 Kenneth Branagh, actor, *Much Ado About Nothing*,
Harry Potter and the Chamber of Secrets
Sun aspects: none
Moon: Virgo   Mercury: Sagittarius   Venus: Aquarius

11 December
1931 Bhagwan Shree Rajneesh, colourful guru with a taste
for Rolls-Royces
Sun aspects: none
Moon: Capricorn   Mercury: Capricorn   Venus: Capricorn

12 December
1915 Frank Sinatra, actor and singer, nicknamed 'Ol' Blue
Eyes'
Sun aspects: none
Moon: Pisces   Mercury: Sagittarius   Venus: Capricorn

13 December
1909 Laurens van der Post, author and mentor of Prince
Charles, *The Seed and the Sower*
Sun aspects: Pluto
Moon: Scorpio   Mercury: Sagittarius   Venus: Sagittarius

14 December

1895 George VI, father of the Queen and husband of the Queen Mother
Sun aspects: Neptune
Moon: Scorpio   Mercury: Sagittarius   Venus: Scorpio

15 December

1892 J. Paul Getty, billionaire oilman, once the world's richest man
Sun aspects: none
Moon: Scorpio   Mercury: Sagittarius   Venus: Scorpio

16 December

1770 Ludwig van Beethoven, one of the greatest composers of all time
Sun aspects: none
Moon: Sagittarius   Mercury: Sagittarius   Venus: Capricorn

17 December

1936 Tommy Steele, entertainer and Britain's first rock 'n' roll star, *Half A Sixpence*
Sun aspects: Saturn, Neptune
Moon: Aquarius   Mercury: Capricorn   Venus: Aquarius

18 December

1946 Steven Spielberg, film director, *Schindler's List*, *E.T.*
Sun aspects: Uranus
Moon: Scorpio   Mercury: Sagittarius   Venus: Scorpio

19 December
1915 Edith Piaf, tragic, self-destructive French singer, 'Milord', 'Non, je ne regrette rien'
Sun aspects: Pluto
Moon: Gemini   Mercury: Sagittarius   Venus: Capricorn

20 December
1946 Uri Geller, psychic with the ability to bend spoons
Sun aspects: Uranus
Moon: Scorpio   Mercury: Sagittarius   Venus: Scorpio

21 December
1937 Jane Fonda, actress, political activist and exercise guru
Sun aspects: Saturn, Neptune
Moon: Leo   Mercury: Capricorn   Venus: Sagittarius

22 December
1949 Maurice and Robin Gibb, musicians of the Bee Gees, 'Tragedy'
Sun aspects: Uranus
Moon: Aquarius   Mercury: Capricorn   Venus: Aquarius

Other Sagittarius people mentioned in this book
Woody Allen, actor and director, *Annie Hall*, *Manhattan* ☆ Joan Armatrading, singer, *Square the Circle* ☆ Jane Austen, author, *Emma*, *Persuasion* ☆ Kim Basinger, actress, *Batman* ☆ Jane Birkin, actress, *Evil Under The Sun* ☆ John Brown, Queen Victoria's Highland servant ☆ Frances Hodgson Burnett, author, *Little Lord Fauntleroy* ☆ Ada Byron, mathematician daughter of Lord Byron ☆ Thomas Carlyle, historian and philosopher, *On Heroes, Hero Worship and the Heroic in History* ☆ Dale Carnegie, inspirational writer, *How to Stop Worrying and Start Living* ☆ King Charles I, beheaded in 1649 after the English Civil War ☆ Jacques Chirac, French

president who continued nuclear testing in the Pacific despite international protests ☆ Arthur C. Clarke, science fiction writer, *2001: A Space Odyssey* ☆ Roberta Close, Brazilian transsexual ☆ Martin Clunes, actor, *Men Behaving Badly* ☆ Ronnie Corbett, comedian, *The Two Ronnies* ☆ Noël Coward, playwright and wit, *Hay Fever, Private Lives* ☆ General George Custer, American Civil War commander ☆ Sammy Davis Jr, singer and actor, *Ocean's Eleven* ☆ Humphrey Davy, inventor of a safety lamp for miners ☆ Emily Dickinson, influential American poet, *Bolts of Melody* ☆ Benjamin Disraeli, flamboyant British prime minister in Victorian times ☆ Otto Dix, German realist painter ☆ Friedrich Engels, socialist thinker, *The Communist Manifesto* ☆ Milton Erickson, hypnotherapist and inspiration for NLP ☆ Franz Ferdinand, Hapsburg Archduke whose assassination led to the outbreak of the First World War ☆ Lucien Freud, British realist painter ☆ Charles Forte, hotel chain magnate ☆ Connie Francis, singer, 'Who's Sorry Now?' ☆ Françoise Gilot, young lover of Pablo Picasso, 42 years his junior ☆ Hermione Gingold, actress and wit, *How to Grow Old Disgracefully* ☆ Jean-Luc Godard, film director, *Breathless* ☆ Jimi Hendrix, musician, 'Purple Haze' ☆ William Hogarth, satirical eighteenth-century morality artist, *A Harlot's Progress* ☆ Gordon Jackson, actor, *Upstairs, Downstairs* ☆ Don Johnson, actor, *Miami Vice* ☆ Curt Jurgens, German actor, *The Spy Who Loved Me* ☆ Petra Kelly, Green Party co-founder ☆ Dorothy Lamour, actress, *The Road to Singapore* ☆ Brenda Lee, singer, 'Nobody Wins' ☆ 'Lucky' Luciano, New York gangster ☆ Alicia Markova, the greatest English classical ballerina before Margot Fonteyn ☆ Margaret Mead, anthropologist, *Coming of Age in Samoa* ☆ Bette Midler, comedian and singer, 'From a Distance' ☆ John Milton, poet, *Lycidas, Paradise Lost* ☆ Nancy Mitford, author, *Love in a Cold Climate, Noblesse Oblige* ☆ Julianne Moore, actress, *Jurassic Park* ☆ Jim Morrison, musician from The Doors, 'Light My Fire' ☆ Edvard Munch, artist, *The Scream* ☆ Dennis

Nilsen, English serial killer of homosexual men ☆ Edna O'Brien, Irish author, *The Country Girls* ☆ Sinead O'Connor, singer, 'Nothing Compares To You' ☆ Christina Onassis, daughter of shipping magnate Aristotle ☆ Ozzy Osbourne, heavy metal singer from Black Sabbath, 'Paranoid' ☆ Donny Osmond, singer, 'Puppy Love' ☆ Pat Phoenix, actress, *Coronation Street* ☆ Brad Pitt, actor, *Fight Club* ☆ Christina Rossetti, poet, 'Goblin Market', 'A Birthday' ☆ Britney Spears, singer, 'Baby One More Time' ☆ Pamela Stephenson, comedian wife of Billy Connolly ☆ Kiefer Sutherland, actor, *A Few Good Men* ☆ Henri de Toulouse-Lautrec, diminutive Parisian painter, *Moulin Rouge* ☆ Joanna Trollope, author, *Other People's Children*, *Next of Kin* ☆ Tina Turner, singer, 'Private Dancer' ☆ Mark Twain, author, *A Tramp Abroad*, *Tom Sawyer* ☆ Gianni Versace, murdered fashion designer ☆ Dionne Warwick, singer, 'Walk On By' ☆ Andy Williams, singer, 'Can't Get Used to Losing You' ☆ Bill Wilson, founder of Alcoholics Anonymous ☆ Frank Zappa, musician from The Mothers of Invention, 'Joe's Garage'.

ELEVEN

Finding Your Sun, Moon, Mercury and Venus Signs

ALL OF THE ASTROLOGICAL DATA IN THIS BOOK WAS CALCULATED by Astrolabe, who also supply a wide range of astrological software. I am most grateful for their help and generosity.

ASTROLABE, PO Box 1750, Brewster, MA 02631, USA
www.alabe.com

PLEASE NOTE THAT ALL OF THE TIMES GIVEN ARE IN GREENWICH MEAN TIME (GMT). If you were born during British Summer Time (BST) you will need to subtract one hour from your birth time to convert it to GMT. If you were born outside of the British Isles, find the time zone of your place of birth and the number of hours it is different from GMT. Add the difference in hours if you were born west of the UK, and subtract the difference if you were born east of the UK to convert your birth time to GMT.

Your Sun Sign

Check your year of birth, and if you were born between the dates and times given the Sun was in Sagittarius when you were born – confirming that you're a Sagittarian. If you were born before the time on the date that Sagittarius begins in your year, you are a Scorpio. If you were born after the time on the date that Sagittarius ends in your year, you are a Capricorn.

Your Moon Sign

The Moon changes sign every two and a half days. To find your Moon sign, first find your year of birth. You will notice that in each year box there are three columns.

The second column shows the day of the month that the Moon changed sign, while the first column gives the abbreviation for the sign that the Moon entered on that date.

In the middle column, the month has been omitted, so that the dates run from, for example, 22 to 30 (November) and then from 1 to 22 (December).

In the third column, after the star, the time that the Moon changed sign on that day is given.

Look down the middle column of your year box to find your date of birth. If your birth date is given, look to the third column to find the time that the Moon changed sign. If you were born after that time, your Moon sign is given in the first column next to your birth date. If you were born before that time, your Moon sign is the one above the one next to your birth date.

If your birth date is not given, find the closest date before it. The sign shown next to that date is your Moon sign.

If you were born on a day that the Moon changed signs and you do not know your time of birth, try out both of that day's Moon signs and feel which one fits you best.

The abbreviations for the signs are as follows:

Aries – Ari   Taurus – Tau   Gemini – Gem   Cancer – Can
Leo – Leo   Virgo – Vir   Libra – Lib   Scorpio – Sco
Sagittarius – Sag Capricorn – Cap   Aquarius – Aqu   Pisces – Pis

Your Mercury Sign

Find your year of birth and then the column in which your birthday falls. Look up to the top of the column to find your Mercury sign. You will see that some dates appear twice. This is because Mercury changed sign that day. If your birthday falls on one of these dates, try out both Mercury signs and see which one fits you best. If you know your birth time, you can find out for sure which Mercury sign is yours on my website – www.janeridderpatrick.com.

Your Venus Sign

Find your year of birth and then the column in which your birthday falls. Look up to the top of the column to find your Venus sign. Some dates have two possible signs. That's because Venus changed signs that day. Try them both out and see which fits you best. If the year you are interested in doesn't appear in the tables, or you have Venus in the same sign as your Sun and want to know whether you have a morning or evening star Venus, you can find the information on my website – www.janeridderpatrick.com.

↗ Sagittarius Sun Tables ☉

YEAR	SAGITTARIUS BEGINS	SAGITTARIUS ENDS
1930	23 Nov 00.34	22 Dec 13.39
1931	23 Nov 06.24	22 Dec 19.29
1932	22 Nov 12.10	22 Dec 01.14
1933	22 Nov 17.53	22 Dec 06.57
1934	22 Nov 23.44	22 Dec 12.49
1935	23 Nov 05.35	22 Dec 18.37
1936	22 Nov 11.25	22 Dec 00.26
1937	22 Nov 17.16	22 Dec 06.21
1938	22 Nov 23.06	22 Dec 12.13
1939	23 Nov 04.58	22 Dec 18.05
1940	22 Nov 10.48	21 Dec 23.54
1941	22 Nov 16.37	22 Dec 05.44
1942	22 Nov 22.30	22 Dec 11.39
1943	23 Nov 04.21	22 Dec 17.29
1944	22 Nov 10.07	21 Dec 23.14
1945	22 Nov 15.55	22 Dec 05.03
1946	22 Nov 21.46	22 Dec 10.53
1947	23 Nov 03.37	22 Dec 16.42
1948	22 Nov 09.28	21 Dec 22.33
1949	22 Nov 15.16	22 Dec 04.22
1950	22 Nov 21.20	22 Dec 10.13
1951	23 Nov 02.51	22 Dec 16.00
1952	22 Nov 08.35	21 Dec 21.43
1953	22 Nov 14.22	22 Dec 03.31
1954	22 Nov 20.14	22 Dec 09.24
1955	23 Nov 02.00	22 Dec 15.10
1956	22 Nov 07.49	21 Dec 20.59
1957	22 Nov 13.39	22 Dec 02.48
1958	22 Nov 19.29	22 Dec 08.39
1959	23 Nov 01.26	22 Dec 14.34
1960	22 Nov 07.18	21 Dec 20.25
1961	22 Nov 13.07	22 Dec 02.19
1962	22 Nov 19.01	22 Dec 08.15
1963	23 Nov 00.49	22 Dec 14.01

YEAR	SAGITTARIUS BEGINS	SAGITTARIUS ENDS
1964	22 Nov 06.38	21 Dec 19.49
1965	22 Nov 12.29	22 Dec 01.40
1966	22 Nov 18.14	22 Dec 07.28
1967	23 Nov 00.04	22 Dec 13.16
1968	22 Nov 05.48	21 Dec 18.59
1969	22 Nov 11.31	22 Dec 00.43
1970	22 Nov 17.24	22 Dec 06.35
1971	22 Nov 05.02	22 Dec 12.23
1972	22 Nov 05.02	21 Dec 18.12
1973	22 Nov 10.54	22 Dec 00.07
1974	22 Nov 16.38	22 Dec 05.55
1975	22 Nov 22.30	22 Dec 11.45
1976	22 Nov 04.21	21 Dec 17.35
1977	22 Nov 10.07	21 Dec 23.23
1978	22 Nov 16.04	22 Dec 05.20
1979	22 Nov 21.54	22 Dec 11.09
1980	22 Nov 03.41	21 Dec 22.50
1981	22 Nov 09.35	21 Dec 22.50
1982	22 Nov 15.23	22 Dec 04.38
1983	22 Nov 21.18	22 Dec 10.29
1984	22 Nov 03.10	21 Dec 16.22
1985	22 Nov 08.50	21 Dec 22.07
1986	22 Nov 14.44	22 Dec 04.02
1987	22 Nov 20.29	22 Dec 09.45
1988	22 Nov 02.11	21 Dec 15.27
1989	22 Nov 08.04	21 Dec 21.21
1990	22 Nov 13.46	22 Dec 03.07
1991	22 Nov 19.35	22 Dec 08.53
1992	22 Nov 01.25	21 Dec 14.43
1993	22 Nov 07.06	21 Dec 20.25
1994	22 Nov 13.05	22 Dec 02.22
1995	22 Nov 19.01	22 Dec 08.16
1996	22 Nov 00.49	21 Dec 14.05
1997	22 Nov 06.47	21 Dec 20.06
1998	22 Nov 12.34	22 Dec 01.56
1999	22 Nov 18.24	22 Dec 07.43
2000	22 Nov 00.19	21 Dec 13.37

♐ Sagittarius – Finding Your Moon Sign ☽

1930
Cap	22	*21:42
Aqu	25	*07:22
Pis	27	*19:32
Ari	30	*08:06
Tau	2	*18:31
Gem	5	*01:30
Can	7	*05:31
Leo	9	*07:52
Vir	11	*10:04
Lib	13	*13:05
Sco	15	*17:19
Sag	17	*22:54
Cap	20	*06:11
Aqu	22	*15:43

1931
Tau	22	*15:59
Gem	25	*03:11
Can	27	*12:08
Leo	29	*19:05
Vir	2	*00:15
Lib	4	*03:43
Sco	6	*05:43
Sag	8	*07:04
Cap	10	*09:18
Aqu	12	*14:10
Pis	14	*22:51
Ari	17	*10:49
Tau	19	*23:44

1932
Lib	23	*15:06
Sco	25	*16:37
Sag	27	*15:58
Cap	29	*15:16
Aqu	1	*16:46
Pis	3	*22:09
Ari	6	*07:35
Tau	8	*19:41
Gem	11	*08:25
Can	13	*20:27
Leo	16	*07:12
Vir	18	*16:08
Lib	20	*22:30

1933
Aqu	22	*01:21
Pis	24	*04:50
Ari	26	*11:13
Tau	28	*20:03
Gem	1	*06:44
Can	3	*18:52
Leo	6	*07:48
Vir	8	*19:59
Lib	11	*05:18
Sco	13	*10:25
Sag	15	*11:47
Cap	17	*11:08
Aqu	19	*10:38
Pis	21	*12:16

1934
Can	23	*16:25
Leo	26	*03:54
Vir	28	*16:51
Lib	1	*04:38
Sco	3	*13:04
Sag	5	*17:52
Cap	7	*20:08
Aqu	9	*21:33
Pis	11	*23:31
Ari	14	*02:51
Tau	16	*07:56
Gem	18	*14:58
Can	21	*00:11

♐ Sagittarius – Finding Your Moon Sign ☽

1935		
Sco	23	*11:35
Sag	25	*21:07
Cap	28	*04:27
Aqu	30	*09:59
Pis	2	*14:02
Ari	4	*16:52
Tau	6	*19:03
Gem	8	*21:37
Can	11	*01:54
Leo	13	*09:07
Vir	15	*19:32
Lib	18	*07:58
Sco	20	*20:02

1936		
Pis	22	*02:02
Ari	24	*05:36
Tau	26	*06:28
Gem	28	*06:11
Can	30	*06:40
Leo	2	*09:44
Vir	4	*16:31
Lib	7	*02:55
Sco	9	*15:27
Sag	12	*04:06
Cap	14	*15:24
Aqu	17	*00:41
Pis	19	*07:43
Ari	21	*12:25

1937		
Leo	22	*15:55
Vir	24	*19:56
Lib	27	*03:22
Sco	29	*13:46
Sag	2	*02:05
Cap	4	*15:07
Aqu	7	*03:39
Pis	9	*14:20
Ari	11	*21:53
Tau	14	*01:48
Gem	16	*02:41
Can	18	*02:02
Leo	20	*01:49

1938		
Sag	22	*01:57
Cap	24	*12:38
Aqu	27	*00:58
Pis	29	*13:29
Ari	2	*00:01
Tau	4	*07:00
Gem	6	*10:17
Can	8	*11:07
Leo	10	*11:17
Vir	12	*12:38
Lib	14	*16:27
Sco	16	*23:13
Sag	19	*08:31
Cap	21	*19:38

1939		
Tau	24	*07:22
Gem	26	*15:08
Can	28	*20:11
Leo	30	*23:33
Vir	3	*02:22
Lib	5	*05:22
Sco	7	*08:57
Sag	9	*13:32
Cap	11	*19:51
Aqu	14	*04:42
Pis	16	*16:14
Ari	19	*05:02
Tau	21	*16:31

♐ Sagittarius – Finding Your Moon Sign ☽

1940		
Vir	22	*16:10
Lib	24	*19:24
Sco	26	*20:44
Sag	28	*21:18
Cap	30	*22:51
Aqu	3	*03:13
Pis	5	*11:36
Ari	7	*23:26
Tau	10	*12:26
Gem	13	*00:06
Can	15	*09:19
Leo	17	*16:15
Vir	19	*21:34

1941		
Aqu	23	*06:46
Pis	25	*12:10
Ari	27	*21:26
Tau	30	*09:18
Gem	2	*21:59
Can	5	*10:21
Leo	7	*21:42
Vir	10	*07:11
Lib	12	*13:44
Sco	14	*16:51
Sag	16	*17:09
Cap	18	*16:26
Aqu	20	*16:53

1942		
Gem	22	*20:34
Can	25	*08:16
Leo	27	*21:09
Vir	30	*09:28
Lib	2	*18:54
Sco	5	*00:04
Sag	7	*01:32
Cap	9	*01:06
Aqu	11	*00:57
Pis	13	*02:56
Ari	15	*08:04
Tau	17	*16:16
Gem	20	*02:46

1943		
Lib	22	*17:18
Sco	25	*02:07
Sag	27	*07:34
Cap	29	*10:42
Aqu	1	*13:01
Pis	3	*15:35
Ari	5	*18:59
Tau	7	*23:30
Gem	10	*05:32
Can	12	*13:47
Leo	15	*00:37
Vir	17	*13:22
Lib	20	*01:54

1944		
Pis	23	*06:18
Ari	25	*08:56
Tau	27	*10:22
Gem	29	*11:55
Can	1	*15:17
Leo	3	*21:53
Vir	6	*08:04
Lib	8	*20:28
Sco	11	*08:41
Sag	13	*18:49
Cap	16	*02:20
Aqu	18	*07:43
Pis	20	*11:38

♐ Sagittarius – Finding Your Moon Sign ☽

1945		
Leo	23	*23:13
Vir	26	*05:59
Lib	28	*16:18
Sco	1	*04:43
Sag	3	*17:29
Cap	6	*05:23
Aqu	8	*15:33
Pis	10	*23:19
Ari	13	*04:14
Tau	15	*06:29
Gem	17	*07:02
Can	19	*07:27
Leo	21	*09:31

1946		
Sag	23	*15:43
Cap	26	*04:39
Aqu	28	*17:29
Pis	1	*04:29
Ari	3	*12:03
Tau	5	*15:47
Gem	7	*16:29
Can	9	*15:49
Leo	11	*15:46
Vir	13	*18:08
Lib	16	*00:08
Sco	18	*09:43
Sag	20	*21:48

1947		
Ari	23	*12:51
Tau	25	*20:05
Gem	27	*23:54
Can	30	*01:30
Leo	2	*02:30
Vir	4	*04:23
Lib	6	*08:14
Sco	8	*14:24
Sag	10	*22:49
Cap	13	*09:14
Aqu	15	*21:15
Pis	18	*09:58
Ari	20	*21:35

1948		
Vir	23	*18:48
Lib	25	*21:32
Sco	28	*00:18
Sag	30	*03:52
Cap	2	*09:17
Aqu	4	*17:31
Pis	7	*04:45
Ari	9	*17:29
Tau	12	*05:08
Gem	14	*13:42
Can	16	*19:00
Leo	18	*22:02
Vir	21	*00:19

1949		
Cap	22	*12:20
Aqu	24	*16:24
Pis	27	*00:36
Ari	29	*12:18
Tau	2	*01:21
Gem	4	*13:27
Can	6	*23:30
Leo	9	*07:27
Vir	11	*13:30
Lib	13	*17:44
Sco	15	*20:13
Sag	17	*21:31
Cap	19	*23:00

♐ Sagittarius – Finding Your Moon Sign ☽

1950		
Gem	24	*11:38
Can	27	*00:12
Leo	29	*12:01
Vir	1	*21:52
Lib	4	*04:28
Sco	6	*07:18
Sag	8	*07:16
Cap	10	*06:16
Aqu	12	*06:34
Pis	14	*10:11
Ari	16	*17:58
Tau	19	*05:09
Gem	21	*17:49

1951		
Lib	24	*08:07
Sco	26	*13:30
Sag	28	*15:19
Cap	30	*15:22
Aqu	2	*15:45
Pis	4	*18:07
Ari	6	*23:18
Tau	9	*07:04
Gem	11	*16:54
Can	14	*04:22
Leo	16	*17:04
Vir	19	*05:52
Lib	21	*16:40

1952		
Aqu	22	*04:51
Pis	24	*07:54
Ari	26	*11:09
Tau	28	*14:54
Gem	30	*19:53
Can	3	*03:09
Leo	5	*13:23
Vir	8	*01:57
Lib	10	*14:34
Sco	13	*00:37
Sag	15	*06:59
Cap	17	*10:16
Aqu	19	*12:02
Pis	21	*13:45

1953		
Can	23	*04:32
Leo	25	*10:41
Vir	27	*20:41
Lib	30	*09:05
Sco	2	*21:29
Sag	5	*08:08
Cap	7	*16:32
Aqu	9	*22:58
Pis	12	*03:45
Ari	14	*07:05
Tau	16	*09:22
Gem	18	*11:27
Can	20	*14:40

1954		
Sco	22	*18:12
Sag	25	*07:01
Cap	27	*19:23
Aqu	30	*06:18
Pis	2	*14:37
Ari	4	*19:34
Tau	6	*21:21
Gem	8	*21:16
Can	10	*21:06
Leo	12	*22:49
Vir	15	*03:54
Lib	17	*12:52
Sco	20	*00:43

♐ Sagittarius – Finding Your Moon Sign ☽

1955		
Pis	22	*18:10
Ari	25	*01:45
Tau	27	*05:26
Gem	29	*06:10
Can	1	*05:46
Leo	3	*06:07
Vir	5	*08:50
Lib	7	*14:48
Sco	10	*00:00
Sag	12	*11:33
Cap	15	*00:23
Aqu	17	*13:18
Pis	20	*01:01

1956		
Leo	22	*18:09
Vir	24	*20:32
Lib	27	*00:11
Sco	29	*05:34
Sag	1	*12:59
Cap	3	*22:36
Aqu	6	*10:16
Pis	8	*22:56
Ari	11	*10:35
Tau	13	*19:14
Gem	16	*00:04
Can	18	*01:51
Leo	20	*02:11

1957		
Cap	23	*22:30
Aqu	26	*06:16
Pis	28	*17:15
Ari	1	*05:56
Tau	3	*17:47
Gem	6	*02:59
Can	8	*09:15
Leo	10	*13:22
Vir	12	*16:28
Lib	14	*19:22
Sco	16	*22:35
Sag	19	*02:30
Cap	21	*07:47

1958		
Tau	23	*14:30
Gem	26	*02:59
Can	28	*13:50
Leo	30	*22:39
Vir	3	*05:17
Lib	5	*09:29
Sco	7	*11:27
Sag	9	*12:01
Cap	11	*12:47
Aqu	13	*15:38
Pis	15	*22:13
Ari	18	*08:45
Tau	20	*21:37

1959		
Vir	23	*12:06
Lib	25	*18:40
Sco	27	*21:20
Sag	29	*21:11
Cap	1	*20:11
Aqu	3	*20:35
Pis	6	*00:17
Ari	8	*07:59
Tau	10	*18:55
Gem	13	*07:24
Can	15	*20:00
Leo	18	*07:57
Vir	20	*18:29

♐ Sagittarius – Finding Your Moon Sign ☽

1960		
Aqu	23	*07:04
Pis	25	*09:50
Ari	27	*14:51
Tau	29	*22:00
Gem	2	*07:00
Can	4	*17:52
Leo	7	*06:20
Vir	9	*19:12
Lib	12	*06:10
Sco	14	*13:11
Sag	16	*16:06
Cap	18	*16:15
Aqu	20	*15:48

1961		
Gem	22	*09:59
Can	24	*16:20
Leo	27	*02:01
Vir	29	*14:25
Lib	2	*03:07
Sco	4	*13:28
Sag	6	*20:23
Cap	9	*00:29
Aqu	11	*03:11
Pis	13	*05:41
Ari	15	*08:44
Tau	17	*12:39
Gem	19	*17:47

1962		
Sco	24	*10:32
Sag	26	*21:42
Cap	29	*07:00
Aqu	1	*14:25
Pis	3	*19:52
Ari	5	*23:16
Tau	8	*00:58
Gem	10	*02:07
Can	12	*04:21
Leo	14	*09:21
Vir	16	*17:59
Lib	19	*05:41
Sco	21	*18:17

1963		
Pis	24	*05:32
Ari	26	*10:23
Tau	28	*11:48
Gem	30	*11:14
Can	2	*10:45
Leo	4	*12:21
Vir	6	*17:26
Lib	9	*02:22
Sco	11	*14:04
Sag	14	*02:53
Cap	16	*15:20
Aqu	19	*02:28
Pis	21	*11:27

1964		
Leo	23	*20:59
Vir	26	*00:03
Lib	28	*05:54
Sco	30	*14:31
Sag	3	*01:24
Cap	5	*13:53
Aqu	8	*02:57
Pis	10	*14:59
Ari	13	*00:10
Tau	15	*05:32
Gem	17	*07:20
Can	19	*07:02
Leo	21	*06:30

↗ Sagittarius – Finding Your Moon Sign ☽

1965		
Sag	23	*02:57
Cap	25	*11:46
Aqu	27	*23:03
Pis	30	*11:39
Ari	2	*23:21
Tau	5	*08:10
Gem	7	*13:26
Can	9	*15:56
Leo	11	*17:07
Vir	13	*18:35
Lib	15	*21:34
Sco	18	*02:40
Sag	20	*10:01

1966		
Ari	22	*18:30
Tau	25	*06:36
Gem	27	*16:30
Can	29	*23:48
Leo	2	*05:01
Vir	4	*08:47
Lib	6	*11:42
Sco	8	*14:17
Sag	10	*17:13
Cap	12	*21:31
Aqu	15	*04:19
Pis	17	*14:17
Ari	20	*02:39

1967		
Leo	22	*13:46
Vir	24	*20:44
Lib	27	*00:46
Sco	29	*02:12
Sag	1	*02:10
Cap	3	*02:25
Aqu	5	*04:57
Pis	7	*11:20
Ari	9	*21:43
Tau	12	*10:31
Gem	14	*23:17
Can	17	*10:22
Leo	19	*19:20

1968		
Cap	22	*10:20
Aqu	24	*11:03
Pis	26	*14:53
Ari	28	*22:26
Tau	1	*08:57
Gem	3	*21:05
Can	6	*09:43
Leo	8	*22:02
Vir	11	*08:58
Lib	13	*17:08
Sco	15	*21:30
Sag	17	*22:26
Cap	19	*21:32
Aqu	21	*21:00

1969		
Gem	23	*20:59
Can	26	*07:10
Leo	28	*19:21
Vir	1	*08:13
Lib	3	*19:16
Sco	6	*02:28
Sag	8	*05:42
Cap	10	*06:20
Aqu	12	*06:27
Pis	14	*07:56
Ari	16	*11:56
Tau	18	*18:35
Gem	21	*03:28

♐ Sagittarius – Finding Your Moon Sign ☽

1970		
Lib	23	*15:38
Sco	26	*02:23
Sag	28	*10:01
Cap	30	*15:05
Aqu	2	*18:44
Pis	4	*21:55
Ari	7	*01:03
Tau	9	*04:24
Gem	11	*08:33
Can	13	*14:32
Leo	15	*23:22
Vir	18	*11:04
Lib	21	*00:00

1971		
Aqu	23	*05:52
Pis	25	*11:46
Ari	27	*15:02
Tau	29	*16:07
Gem	1	*16:25
Can	3	*17:50
Leo	5	*22:18
Vir	8	*06:40
Lib	10	*18:19
Sco	13	*07:01
Sag	15	*18:37
Cap	18	*04:06
Aqu	20	*11:31

1972		
Can	23	*00:31
Leo	25	*02:12
Vir	27	*07:24
Lib	29	*16:15
Sco	2	*03:42
Sag	4	*16:22
Cap	7	*05:06
Aqu	9	*16:53
Pis	12	*02:31
Ari	14	*08:58
Tau	16	*11:57
Gem	18	*12:23
Can	20	*11:57

1973		
Sco	22	*05:06
Sag	24	*15:11
Cap	27	*03:12
Aqu	29	*16:17
Pis	2	*04:31
Ari	4	*13:48
Tau	6	*19:07
Gem	8	*20:57
Can	10	*20:51
Leo	12	*20:44
Vir	14	*22:21
Lib	17	*02:54
Sco	19	*10:44
Sag	21	*21:20

1974		
Pis	22	*00:10
Ari	24	*11:57
Tau	26	*21:03
Gem	29	*02:57
Can	1	*06:21
Leo	3	*08:31
Vir	5	*10:40
Lib	7	*13:42
Sco	9	*18:13
Sag	12	*00:35
Cap	14	*09:04
Aqu	16	*19:48
Pis	19	*08:11
Ari	21	*20:34

Sagittarius – Finding Your Moon Sign ☽

1975		
Leo	23	*20:47
Vir	26	*01:03
Lib	28	*03:47
Sco	30	*05:36
Sag	2	*07:33
Cap	4	*10:59
Aqu	6	*17:12
Pis	9	*02:52
Ari	11	*15:06
Tau	14	*03:38
Gem	16	*14:11
Can	18	*21:48
Leo	21	*02:53

1976		
Cap	23	*16:03
Aqu	25	*18:29
Pis	28	*00:48
Ari	30	*11:02
Tau	2	*23:41
Gem	5	*12:37
Can	8	*00:20
Leo	10	*10:11
Vir	12	*17:54
Lib	14	*23:12
Sco	17	*02:00
Sag	19	*02:53
Cap	21	*03:11

1977		
Tau	22	*23:09
Gem	25	*10:48
Can	27	*23:19
Leo	30	*11:52
Vir	2	*23:04
Lib	5	*07:16
Sco	7	*11:31
Sag	9	*12:20
Cap	11	*11:25
Aqu	13	*11:00
Pis	15	*13:10
Ari	17	*19:11
Tau	20	*04:54

1978		
Vir	22	*20:56
Lib	25	*08:06
Sco	27	*15:37
Sag	29	*19:22
Cap	1	*20:43
Aqu	3	*21:35
Pis	5	*23:37
Ari	8	*03:40
Tau	10	*09:50
Gem	12	*17:54
Can	15	*03:50
Leo	17	*15:37
Vir	20	*04:34

1979		
Cap	22	*06:01
Aqu	24	*10:36
Pis	26	*14:16
Ari	28	*17:16
Tau	30	*19:54
Gem	2	*23:02
Can	5	*04:02
Leo	7	*12:09
Vir	9	*23:33
Lib	12	*12:28
Sco	15	*00:06
Sag	17	*08:35
Cap	19	*13:53
Aqu	21	*17:12

1980		
Gem	22	*06:27
Can	24	*07:18
Leo	26	*11:24
Vir	28	*19:37
Lib	1	*07:13
Sco	3	*19:59
Sag	6	*07:57
Cap	8	*18:11
Aqu	11	*02:35
Pis	13	*09:02
Ari	15	*13:20
Tau	17	*15:35
Gem	19	*16:39
Can	21	*18:02

1981		
Sco	23	*17:36
Sag	26	*06:00
Cap	28	*18:52
Aqu	1	*07:08
Pis	3	*17:15
Ari	5	*23:47
Tau	8	*02:30
Gem	10	*02:29
Can	12	*01:40
Leo	14	*02:09
Vir	16	*05:38
Lib	18	*12:58
Sco	20	*23:39

1982		
Pis	23	*17:42
Ari	26	*03:05
Tau	28	*08:30
Gem	30	*10:34
Can	2	*10:57
Leo	4	*11:26
Vir	6	*13:33
Lib	8	*18:10
Sco	11	*01:35
Sag	13	*11:27
Cap	15	*23:15
Aqu	18	*12:12
Pis	21	*00:55

1983		
Can	22	*21:10
Leo	25	*00:19
Vir	27	*03:01
Lib	29	*05:56
Sco	1	*09:41
Sag	3	*14:56
Cap	5	*22:28
Aqu	8	*08:39
Pis	10	*20:52
Ari	13	*09:16
Tau	15	*19:32
Gem	18	*02:22
Can	20	*06:02

1984		
Sag	22	*21:34
Cap	25	*00:18
Aqu	27	*06:05
Pis	29	*15:33
Ari	2	*03:42
Tau	4	*16:20
Gem	7	*03:23
Can	9	*11:55
Leo	11	*18:08
Vir	13	*22:34
Lib	16	*01:51
Sco	18	*04:27
Sag	20	*06:58

↗ Sagittarius – Finding Your Moon Sign ☽

1985			1986			1987			1988			1989		
Ari	22	*00:43	Leo	22	*01:24	Cap	23	*11:31	Gem	23	*13:12	Lib	22	*20:25
Tau	24	*13:06	Vir	24	*12:44	Aqu	25	*13:12	Can	25	*17:19	Sco	25	*09:12
Gem	27	*02:07	Lib	26	*20:57	Pis	27	*15:40	Leo	28	*00:52	Sag	27	*21:29
Can	29	*14:22	Sco	29	*01:11	Ari	29	*19:36	Vir	30	*12:00	Cap	30	*08:25
Leo	2	*00:58	Sag	1	*02:07	Tau	2	*01:06	Lib	3	*00:55	Aqu	2	*17:41
Vir	4	*09:13	Cap	3	*01:28	Gem	4	*08:13	Sco	5	*12:50	Pis	5	*00:46
Lib	6	*14:32	Aqu	5	*01:23	Can	6	*17:20	Sag	7	*21:54	Ari	7	*05:11
Sco	8	*16:56	Pis	7	*03:49	Leo	9	*04:40	Cap	10	*04:06	Tau	9	*06:58
Sag	10	*17:13	Ari	9	*09:49	Vir	11	*17:30	Aqu	12	*08:25	Gem	11	*07:14
Cap	12	*16:59	Tau	11	*19:10	Lib	14	*05:39	Pis	14	*11:52	Can	13	*07:49
Aqu	14	*18:14	Gem	14	*06:41	Sco	16	*14:39	Ari	16	*15:03	Leo	15	*10:42
Pis	16	*22:51	Can	16	*19:09	Sag	18	*19:32	Tau	18	*18:10	Vir	17	*17:19
Ari	19	*07:36	Leo	19	*07:43	Cap	20	*21:07	Gem	20	*21:43	Lib	20	*03:45
Tau	21	*19:40	Vir	21	*19:30									

♐ Sagittarius – Finding Your Moon Sign ☽

1990		
Aqu	22	*21:06
Pis	25	*07:31
Ari	27	*14:04
Tau	29	*16:36
Gem	1	*16:22
Can	3	*15:27
Leo	5	*16:00
Vir	7	*19:39
Lib	10	*03:00
Sco	12	*13:28
Sag	15	*01:43
Cap	17	*14:34
Aqu	20	*02:58

1991		
Gem	22	*00:21
Can	24	*01:25
Leo	26	*02:37
Vir	28	*05:12
Lib	30	*09:47
Sco	2	*16:33
Sag	5	*01:32
Cap	7	*12:41
Aqu	10	*01:26
Pis	12	*14:18
Ari	15	*01:05
Tau	17	*08:08
Gem	19	*11:20
Can	21	*11:54

1992		
Sco	22	*00:52
Sag	24	*05:01
Cap	26	*11:39
Aqu	28	*21:19
Pis	1	*09:23
Ari	3	*21:48
Tau	6	*08:15
Gem	8	*15:35
Can	10	*20:04
Leo	12	*22:46
Vir	15	*00:56
Lib	17	*03:33
Sco	19	*07:19
Sag	21	*12:43

1993		
Ari	23	*16:30
Tau	26	*05:13
Gem	28	*16:47
Can	1	*02:16
Leo	3	*09:32
Vir	5	*14:42
Lib	7	*18:03
Sco	9	*20:04
Sag	11	*21:39
Cap	14	*00:06
Aqu	16	*04:51
Pis	18	*12:59
Ari	21	*00:19

1994		
Leo	23	*15:32
Vir	26	*00:07
Lib	28	*05:21
Sco	30	*07:21
Sag	2	*07:12
Cap	4	*06:42
Aqu	6	*07:52
Pis	8	*12:25
Ari	10	*21:04
Tau	13	*08:56
Gem	15	*21:59
Can	18	*10:24
Leo	20	*21:12

↗ Sagittarius – Finding Your Moon Sign ☽

1995			1996			1997			1998			1999			2000		
Sag	22	*15:55	Tau	22	*16:12	Vir	22	*00:33	Aqu	24	*08:42	Gem	23	*06:13	Sco	23	*07:33
Cap	24	*15:48	Gem	24	*22:20	Lib	24	*13:29	Pis	26	*16:13	Can	25	*05:28	Sag	25	*15:33
Aqu	26	*16:15	Can	27	*06:37	Sco	27	*01:42	Ari	28	*20:32	Leo	27	*06:18	Cap	28	*01:57
Pis	28	*18:59	Leo	29	*17:29	Sag	29	*11:27	Tau	30	*21:51	Vir	29	*10:12	Aqu	30	*14:26
Ari	1	*00:51	Vir	2	*06:10	Cap	1	*18:38	Gem	2	*21:29	Lib	1	*17:29	Pis	3	*03:22
Tau	3	*09:40	Lib	4	*18:23	Aqu	3	*23:57	Can	4	*21:28	Sco	4	*03:35	Ari	5	*14:16
Gem	5	*20:34	Sco	7	*03:37	Pis	6	*04:06	Leo	6	*23:56	Sag	6	*15:27	Tau	7	*21:25
Can	8	*08:44	Sag	9	*08:57	Ari	8	*07:23	Vir	9	*06:21	Cap	9	*04:13	Gem	10	*00:49
Leo	10	*21:24	Cap	11	*11:13	Tau	10	*09:59	Lib	11	*16:43	Aqu	11	*16:58	Can	12	*01:48
Vir	13	*09:25	Aqu	13	*12:14	Gem	12	*12:35	Sco	14	*05:16	Pis	14	*04:17	Leo	14	*02:08
Lib	15	*19:08	Pis	15	*13:44	Can	14	*16:25	Sag	16	*17:47	Ari	16	*12:28	Vir	16	*03:30
Sco	18	*01:05	Ari	17	*16:55	Leo	16	*22:58	Cap	19	*04:54	Tau	18	*16:44	Lib	18	*07:01
Sag	20	*03:12	Tau	19	*22:10	Vir	19	*09:00	Aqu	21	*14:16	Gem	20	*17:38	Sco	20	*13:12
						Lib	21	*21:34									

✒ Sagittarius Mercury Signs ☿

YEAR	SCORPIO	SAGITTARIUS	CAPRICORN
1930		22 Nov–6 Dec	6 Dec–22 Dec
1931		22 Nov–2 Dec	2 Dec–20 Dec
		20 Dec–22 Dec	
1932	22 Nov–22 Dec		
1933	22 Nov–12 Dec	12 Dec–22 Dec	
1934	22 Nov–6 Dec	6 Dec–22 Dec	
1935		22 Nov–18 Dec	18 Dec–22 Dec
1936		22 Nov–10 Dec	10 Dec–22 Dec
1937		22 Nov–3 Dec	3 Dec–22 Dec
1938		22 Nov–22 Dec	
1939	3 Dec–13 Dec	22 Nov–3 Dec	
		13 Dec–22 Dec	
1940	22 Nov–9 Dec	9 Dec–22 Dec	
1941	22 Nov–3 Dec	3 Dec–22 Dec	
1942	22 Nov–25 Nov	25 Nov–14 Dec	14 Dec–22 Dec
1943		22 Nov–8 Dec	8 Dec–22 Dec
1944		22 Nov–1 Dec	1 Dec–22 Dec
1945		22 Nov–22 Dec	
1946	22 Nov–12 Dec	12 Dec–22 Dec	
1947	22 Nov–7 Dec	7 Dec–22 Dec	
1948	22 Nov–29 Nov	29 Nov–18 Dec	18 Dec–22 Dec
1949		22 Nov–11 Dec	11 Dec–22 Dec
1950		22 Nov–5 Dec	5 Dec–22 Dec
1951		22 Nov–1 Dec	1 Dec–12 Dec
		12 Dec–22 Dec	
1952		22 Nov–22 Dec	
1953	22 Nov–10 Dec	10 Dec–22 Dec	
1954	22 Nov–4 Dec	4 Dec–22 Dec	
1955	22 Nov–27 Nov	27 Nov–16 Dec	16 Dec–22 Dec

YEAR	SCORPIO	SAGITTARIUS	CAPRICORN
1956		22 Nov–8 Dec	8 Dec–22 Dec
1957		22 Nov–2 Dec	2 Dec–22 Dec
1958		22 Nov–22 Dec	
1959	25 Nov–13 Dec	22 Nov–25 Nov	
		13 Dec–22 Dec	
1960	22 Nov–7 Dec	7 Dec–22 Dec	
1961	22 Nov–30 Nov	30 Nov–20 Dec	20 Dec–22 Dec
1962	22 Nov–23 Nov	23 Nov–12 Dec	12 Dec–22 Dec
1963		22 Nov–6 Dec	6 Dec–22 Dec
1964		22 Nov–30 Nov	30 Nov–16 Dec
		16 Dec–22 Dec	
1965		22 Nov–22 Dec	
1966	22 Nov–11 Dec	11 Dec–22 Dec	
1967	22 Nov–5 Dec	5 Dec–22 Dec	
1968	22 Nov–27 Nov	27 Nov–16 Dec	16 Dec–22 Dec
1969		22 Nov–9 Dec	9 Dec–22 Dec
1970		22 Nov–3 Dec	3 Dec–22 Dec
1971		22 Nov–22 Dec	
1972	29 Nov–12 Dec	22 Nov–29 Nov	
		12 Dec–22 Dec	
1973	22 Nov–8 Dec	8 Dec–22 Dec	
1974	22 Nov–2 Dec	2 Dec–22 Dec	22 Dec
1975	22 Nov–25 Nov	25 Nov–14 Dec	14 Dec–22 Dec
1976		22 Nov–6 Dec	6 Dec–22 Dec
1977		22 Nov–1 Dec	1 Dec–21 Dec
		21 Dec	
1978		22 Nov–22 Dec	
1979	22 Nov–5 Dec	5 Dec–22 Dec	
1980	22 Nov–5 Dec	5 Dec–22 Dec	
1981	22 Nov–28 Nov	28 Nov–17 Dec	17 Dec–22 Dec
1982		22 Nov–10 Dec	10 Dec–22 Dec
1983		22 Nov–4 Dec	4 Dec–22 Dec

YEAR	SCORPIO	SAGITTARIUS	CAPRICORN
1984		22 Nov–1 Dec	1 Dec–7 Dec
		7 Dec–22 Dec	
1985	4 Dec–12 Dec	22 Nov–4 Dec	
		12 Dec–22 Dec	
1986	22 Nov–10 Dec	10 Dec–22 Dec	
1987	22 Nov–3 Dec	3 Dec–22 Dec	
1988	22 Nov–25 Nov	25 Nov–14 Dec	14 Dec–22 Dec
1989		22 Nov–7 Dec	7 Dec–22 Dec
1990		22 Nov–2 Dec	2 Dec–22 Dec
1991		22 Nov–22 Dec	
1992	22 Nov–12 Dec	12 Dec–22 Dec	
1993	22 Nov–7 Dec	7 Dec–22 Dec	
1994	22 Nov–30 Nov	30 Nov–19 Dec	19 Dec–22 Dec
1995		22 Nov–12 Dec	12 Dec–22 Dec
1996		22 Nov–4 Dec	4 Dec–22 Dec
1997		22 Nov–30 Nov	30 Nov–13 Dec
		13 Dec–22 Dec	
1998		22 Nov–22 Dec	
1999	22 Nov–11 Dec	11 Dec–22 Dec	
2000	22 Nov–3 Dec	3 Dec–22 Dec	

Sagittarius Venus Signs 1930–2000 ♀

YEAR	LIBRA	SCORPIO	SAGITTARIUS	CAPRICORN	AQUARIUS
1930		22 Nov–22 Dec	22 Dec		
1931			22 Nov–1 Dec	1 Dec–22 Dec	
1932	22 Nov–27 Nov	27 Nov–22 Dec	22 Dec		
1933				22 Nov–5 Dec	5 Dec–22 Dec
1934		22 Nov	22 Nov–16 Dec	16 Dec–22 Dec	
1935	22 Nov–8 Dec	8 Dec–22 Dec			
1936				22 Nov–6 Dec	6 Dec–22 Dec
1937		22 Nov–6 Dec	6 Dec–22 Dec		
1938		22 Nov–22 Dec			
1939			22 Nov–1 Dec	1 Dec–22 Dec	
1940		22 Nov–26 Nov	26 Nov–20 Dec	20 Dec–22 Dec	
1941				22 Nov–5 Dec	5 Dec–22 Dec
1942			22 Nov–15 Dec	15 Dec–22 Dec	
1943	22 Nov–8 Dec	8 Dec–22 Dec			
1944				22 Nov–11 Dec	11 Dec–22 Dec
1945		22 Nov–6 Dec	6 Dec–22 Dec		
1946			22 Nov–22 Dec		
1947			22 Nov–30 Nov	30 Nov–22 Dec	
1948	22 Nov–26 Nov	26 Nov–20 Dec	20 Dec–22 Dec		
1949				22 Nov–6 Dec	6 Dec–22 Dec
1950			22 Nov–14 Dec	14 Dec–22 Dec	
1951	22 Nov–8 Dec	8 Dec–22 Dec			

YEAR	LIBRA	SCORPIO	SAGITTARIUS	CAPRICORN	AQUARIUS
1952		22 Nov–5 Dec	5 Dec–22 Dec	22 Nov–10 Dec	10 Dec–22 Dec
1953		22 Nov–22 Dec			
1954					
1955			22 Nov–30 Nov	30 Nov–22 Dec	
1956	22 Nov–25 Nov	25 Nov–19 Dec	19 Dec–22 Dec		6 Dec–22 Dec
1957				22 Nov–6 Dec	
1958				14 Dec–22 Dec	
1959			22 Nov–14 Dec		10 Dec–22 Dec
1960	22 Nov–7 Dec	7 Dec–22 Dec		22 Nov–10 Dec	
1961		22 Nov–5 Dec	5 Dec–22 Dec		
1962		22 Nov–22 Dec			
1963			22 Nov–29 Nov	29 Nov–22 Dec	
1964	22 Nov–25 Nov	25 Nov–19 Dec	19 Dec–22 Dec		7 Dec–22 Dec
1965				22 Nov–7 Dec	
1966				13 Dec–22 Dec	
1967	22 Nov–7 Dec	7 Dec–22 Dec	22 Nov–13 Dec		
1968				22 Nov–9 Dec	9 Dec–22 Dec
1969		22 Nov–4 Dec	4 Dec–22 Dec		
1970		22 Nov–22 Dec			
1971			22 Nov–29 Nov	29 Nov–22 Dec	
1972	22 Nov–24 Nov	24 Nov–18 Dec	18 Dec–22 Dec		7 Dec–22 Dec
1973				22 Nov–7 Dec	
1974				13 Dec–22 Dec	
1975	22 Nov–7 Dec	7 Dec–22 Dec	22 Nov–13 Dec		
1976				22 Nov–9 Dec	9 Dec–22 Dec

YEAR	LIBRA	SCORPIO	SAGITTARIUS	CAPRICORN	AQUARIUS
1977		22 Nov–4 Dec	4 Dec–22 Dec		
1978		22 Nov–22 Dec			
1979			22 Nov–28 Nov	28 Nov–22 Dec	
1980	22 Nov–24 Nov	24 Nov–18 Dec	18 Dec–22 Dec		
1981				22 Nov–8 Dec	8 Dec–22 Dec
1982	22 Nov–6 Dec	6 Dec–22 Dec			
1983			22 Nov–12 Dec	12 Dec–22 Dec	
1984				22 Nov–9 Dec	9 Dec–22 Dec
1985		22 Nov–3 Dec	3 Dec–22 Dec		
1986		22 Nov–22 Dec			
1987			22 Nov–28 Nov	28 Nov–22 Dec	
1988	22 Nov–23 Nov	23 Nov–17 Dec	17 Dec–22 Dec		
1989				22 Nov–10 Dec	10 Dec–22 Dec
1990			22 Nov–12 Dec	12 Dec–22 Dec	
1991	22 Nov–6 Dec	6 Dec–22 Dec			
1992				22 Nov–8 Dec	8 Dec–22 Dec
1993		22 Nov–2 Dec	2 Dec–22 Dec		
1994		22 Nov–22 Dec			
1995			22 Nov–23 Nov	23 Nov–17 Dec	17 Dec–22 Dec
1996	22 Nov–23 Nov	23 Nov–17 Dec	17 Dec–22 Dec		
1997				22 Nov–12 Dec	12 Dec–22 Dec
1998			22 Nov–11 Dec	11 Dec–22 Dec	
1999	22 Nov–5 Dec	5 Dec–22 Dec			
2000				22 Nov–8 Dec	8 Dec–22 Dec

The Sagittarius Workbook

There are no right or wrong answers in this chapter. Its aim is to help you assess how you are doing with your life – in YOUR estimation – and to make the material of this book more personal and, I hope, more helpful for you.

1. The Sagittarius in You

Which of the following Sagittarius characteristics do you recognise in yourself?

adventurous	entertaining	enthusiastic
entrepreneurial	freedom-loving	generous
inspirational	lucky	optimistic
philosophical	gregarious	visionary

2. In which situations do you find yourself acting like this?

_____

_____

3. When you are feeling vulnerable, you may show some of the less constructive Sagittarius traits. Do you recognise yourself in any of the following?

clumsy	self-righteous	pontificating
opportunistic	tactless	exaggerative
over-confident	irresponsible	slapdash

What kind of situations trigger off this behaviour and what do you think might help you, in these situations, to respond more positively?

_____

_____

4. You and Your Roles
a) Where, if anywhere, in your life do you play the role of Adventurer?

_____

_____

b) What possibilities do you explore?

_____

_____

5. Do you play any of the following roles – in the literal or broad sense – in any part of your life? If not, would you like to? What might be your first step towards doing so?

Entrepreneur   Philanthropist   Philosopher
Coach   Preacher   Publicist

_____

_____

6. Sun Aspects
If any of the following planets aspects your Sun, add each of the keywords for that planet to complete the following sentences. Which phrases ring true for you?

I am _____

My father is _____

My job requires that I am _____

Saturn Words (Use only if your Sun is aspected by Saturn)

ambitious	controlling	judgmental	mature
serious	strict	traditional	bureaucratic
cautious	committed	hard-working	disciplined
depressive	responsible	status-seeking	limiting

Uranus Words (Use only if your Sun is aspected by Uranus)

freedom-loving	progressive	rebellious	shocking
scientific	cutting-edge	detached	contrary
friendly	disruptive	eccentric	humanitarian
innovative	nonconformist	unconventional	exciting

Neptune Words (Use only if your Sun is aspected by Neptune)

sensitive	idealistic	artistic	impressionable
disappointing	impractical	escapist	self-sacrificing
spiritual	unrealistic	dreamy	glamorous
dependent	deceptive	rescuing	blissful

Pluto Words (Use only if your Sun is aspected by Pluto)

powerful	single-minded	intense	extreme
secretive	rotten	passionate	mysterious
investigative	uncompromising	ruthless	wealthy
abusive	regenerative	associated with sex, birth or death	

a) If one or more negative words describe you or your job, how might you turn that quality into something more positive or satisfying?

_____

_____

7. The Moon and You

Below are brief lists of what the Moon needs, in the various elements, to feel secure and satisfied. First find your Moon element, then estimate how much of each of the following you are expressing and receiving in your life, especially at home and in your relationships, on a scale of 0 to 5 where 0 = none and 5 = plenty.

FIRE MOONS — Aries, Leo, Sagittarius

attention	action	drama
recognition	self-expression	spontaneity
enthusiasm	adventure	leadership

EARTH MOONS — Taurus, Virgo, Capricorn

stability	orderly routine	sensual pleasures
material security	a sense of rootedness	control over your home life
regular body care	practical achievements	pleasurable practical tasks

AIR MOONS — Gemini, Libra, Aquarius

mental rapport	stimulating ideas	emotional space
friendship	social justice	interesting conversations
fairness	socialising	freedom to circulate

WATER MOONS — Cancer, Scorpio, Pisces

intimacy	a sense of belonging	emotional rapport
emotional safety	respect for your feelings	time and space to retreat
acceptance	cherishing and being cherished	warmth and comfort

a) Do you feel your Moon is being 'fed' enough?

yes _____ no _____

b) How might you satisfy your Moon needs even better?

_____

_____

8. You and Your Mercury

As a Sagittarian, your Mercury can only be in Scorpio, Sagittarius or Capricorn. Below are some of the ways and situations in which Mercury in each of the elements might learn and communicate effectively. First find your Mercury sign, then circle the words you think apply to you.

Mercury in Fire (Sagittarius)

action	imagination	identifying with the subject matter
excitement	drama	playing with possibilities

Mercury in Earth (Capricorn)

time-tested methods	useful facts	well-structured information
'how to' instructions	demonstrations	hands-on experience

Mercury in Air (As a Sagittarian, you can never have Mercury in a water sign; the words are included here for completeness)

facts arranged in categories	logic	demonstrable connections
rational arguments	theories	debate and sharing of ideas

Mercury in Water (Scorpio)

pictures and images	charged atmospheres	feeling-linked information
intuitive understanding	emotional rapport	being shown personally

a) This game with Mercury can be done with a friend or on your own. Skim through a magazine until you find a picture that interests you. Then describe the picture – to your friend, or in writing or on tape. Notice what you emphasise and the kind of words you use. Now try to describe it using the language and emphasis of each of the other Mercury modes. How easy did you find that? Identifying the preferred Mercury style of others and using that style yourself can lead to improved communication all round.

9. Your Venus Values
Below are lists of qualities and situations that your Venus sign might enjoy. Assess on a scale of 0 to 5 how much your Venus desires and pleasures are met and expressed in your life. 0 = not at all, 5 = fully.

Venus in Libra
You will activate your Venus through anything cultured, balanced and fair, for example:

harmonious relationships	elegant surroundings	dressing well
courteous manners	artistic pursuits	political justice

Venus in Scorpio
You will activate your Venus through anything that allows you to penetrate to the heart of life's mysteries, for example:

survival situations	money, power and sex	investigating secrets
transformative experiences	recycling	intense relationships

Venus in Sagittarius

You will activate your Venus through following your adventurous spirit, opening up new frontiers and sharing your enthusiasm with others, for example:

travelling	sport	searching for the meaning of life
teaching or preaching	inspiring others	publishing or broadcasting

Venus in Capricorn

You will activate your Venus through anything that makes you feel a respected member of the community, for example:

doing your duty	upholding tradition	working towards goals
achieving ambitions	heading a dynasty	acquiring social status

Venus in Aquarius

You will activate your Venus through freedom from the restraints of convention, for example:

sharing progressive ideas	unusual relationships	noncomformity
humanitarian projects	teamwork	eccentric fashions

a) How, and where, might you have more fun and pleasure by bringing more of what your Venus sign loves into your life?

_____

_____

b) Make a note here of the kind of gifts your Venus sign would love to receive. Then go on and spoil yourself . . .

_____

_____

Resources

Finding an Astrologer

I'm often asked what is the best way to find a reputable astrologer. Personal recommendation by someone whose judgement you trust is by far the best way. Ideally, the astrologer should also be endorsed by a reputable organisation whose members adhere to a strict code of ethics, which guarantees confidentiality and professional conduct.

Contact Addresses

Association of Professional Astrologers
www.professionalastrologers.org

APA members adhere to a strict code of professional ethics.

Astrological Association of Great Britain
www.astrologicalassociation.co.uk

The main body for astrology in the UK that also has information on astrological events and organisations throughout the world.

Faculty of Astrological Studies
www.astrology.org.uk

The teaching body internationally recognised for excellence in astrological education at all levels.

Your Sagittarian Friends

You can keep a record of Sagittarians you know here, with the page numbers of where to find their descriptions handy for future reference.

Name _____   Date of Birth _____
Aspects★   None   Saturn   Uranus   Neptune   Pluto
Moon Sign _____   p _____
Mercury Sign _____   p _____
Venus Sign _____   p _____

Name _____   Date of Birth _____
Aspects★   None   Saturn   Uranus   Neptune   Pluto
Moon Sign _____   p _____
Mercury Sign _____   p _____
Venus Sign _____   p _____

Name _____   Date of Birth _____
Aspects★   None   Saturn   Uranus   Neptune   Pluto
Moon Sign _____   p _____
Mercury Sign _____   p _____
Venus Sign _____   p _____

Name _____   Date of Birth _____
Aspects★   None   Saturn   Uranus   Neptune   Pluto
Moon Sign _____   p _____
Mercury Sign _____   p _____
Venus Sign _____   p _____

★ Circle where applicable

Sign Summaries

SIGN	GLYPH	APPROX DATES	SYMBOL	ROLE	ELEMENT	QUALITY	PLANET	GLYPH	KEYWORD
1. Aries	♈	21/3 – 19/4	Ram	Hero	Fire	Cardinal	Mars	♂	Assertiveness
2. Taurus	♉	20/4 – 20/5	Bull	Steward	Earth	Fixed	Venus	♀	Stability
3. Gemini	♊	21/5 – 21/6	Twins	Go-Between	Air	Mutable	Mercury	☿	Communication
4. Cancer	♋	22/6 – 22/7	Crab	Caretaker	Water	Cardinal	Moon	☽	Nurture
5. Leo	♌	23/7 – 22/8	Lion	Performer	Fire	Fixed	Sun	☉	Glory
6. Virgo	♍	23/8 – 22/9	Maiden	Craftworker	Earth	Mutable	Mercury	☿	Skill
7. Libra	♎	23/9 – 22/10	Scales	Architect	Air	Cardinal	Venus	♀	Balance
8. Scorpio	♏	23/10 – 23/11	Scorpion	Survivor	Water	Fixed	Pluto	♇	Transformation
9. Sagittarius	♐	22/11 – 21/12	Archer	Adventurer	Fire	Mutable	Jupiter	♃	Wisdom
10. Capricorn	♑	22/12 – 19/1	Goat	Manager	Earth	Cardinal	Saturn	♄	Responsibility
11. Aquarius	♒	20/1 – 19/2	Waterbearer	Scientist	Air	Fixed	Uranus	♅	Progress
12. Pisces	♓	20/2 – 20/3	Fishes	Dreamer	Water	Mutable	Neptune	♆	Universality